The Constitution of
The State of Mississippi:
A Quick Reference Guide

Bootblack Budget Books
Copyright 2018 ©
ISBN-13: 978-1986799911
ISBN-10: 1986799913

Contents:

Preamble – Page 27

      Article I: Distribution of Powers – Page 28

Section 1. Powers of Government

Section 2. Encroachment of Power

Article II: Boundaries of the State – Page 29

Section 3. Repealed

Section 4. Acquisition of Territory; Disputed Boundaries

Article III: Bill of Rights – Page 30

SECTION 5. Government Originating in the People

SECTION 6. Regulation of Government; Right to Alter

SECTION 7. Secession Prohibited

SECTION 8. Citizens of State

Section 9. Subordination of Military to Civil Power

Section 10. Treason

Section 11. Peaceful Assemblage; Right to Petition Government

Section 12. Right to Bear Arms

Section 13. Freedom of Speech and Press; Libel

Section 14. Due Process

Section 15. Slavery and Involuntary Servitude Prohibited; Punishment for Crime

Section 16. Ex Post Facto Laws; Impairment of Contract

Section 17. Taking Property for Public Use; Due Compensation

Section 17-A. Taking Private Property by Eminent Domain; Transfer to Others Prohibited for Ten Years; Exceptions

Section 18. Freedom of Religion

Section 19. Repealed

Section 20. Specific Term of Office

Section 21. Writ of Habeas Corpus

Section 22. Double Jeopardy

Section 23. Searches and Seizures

Section 24. Open Courts; Remedy for Injury

Section 25. Access to Courts

Section 26. Rights of Accused; State Grand Jury Proceedings

Section 26-A. Victims Rights; Construction of Provisions; Legislative Authority

Section 27. Proceeding by Indictment or Information

Section 28. Cruel or Unusual Punishment Prohibited

Section 29. Excessive Bail Prohibited; Revocation or Denial of Bail

Section 30. Imprisonment for Debt

Section 31. Trial by Jury. Bill of Rights

Section 32. Construction of Enumerated Rights

Article IV: Legislative Department – Page 39

IN GENERAL

Section 33. Composition of Legislature

Section 34. Composition of House of Representatives

Section 35. Composition of Senate

Section 36. Sessions

Section 37. Elections for Members

Section 38. Election of Officers by Each House

Section 39. President Pro Tempore of Senate

QUALIFICATIONS AND PRIVILEGES OF LEGISLATORS

Section 40. Oath of Office

Section 41. Qualifications of House of Representatives Members

Section 42. Qualifications of Senators

Section 43. Person Liable for Public Monies Ineligible for Office

Section 44. Ineligibility for Office of Person Convicted of Certain Crimes

Section 45. Member Eligibility for Offices Created During Term of Office

Section 46. Salaries of Members

Section 47. Fees or Rewards Prohibited

Section 48. Immunity of Members From Arrest for Certain Crimes

Section 49. Power of Impeachment

Section 50. Impeachment Grounds

Section 51. Removal From Office

Section 52. Persons to Preside in Impeachment Proceedings

Section 53. Removal of Judges for Reasonable Cause

RULES OF PROCEDURE

Section 54. Quorum

Section 55. Determination of Rules by Each House

Section 56. Style of Laws

Section 57. Adjournments; Meeting Place

Section 58. Open Door Policy; Disorderly Behavior

Section 59. Introduction and Passage of Bills

Section 60. Amendment of Bill; Orders, Votes and Resolutions

Section 61. Amendment or Revival by Reference to Title Prohibited

Section 62. Voting On Amendments; Adoption of Committee Reports

Section 63. Maximum Sum Fixed in Appropriation Bill

Section 64. Time Limit and Voting Requirements for Appropriations

Section 65. Reconsideration of Votes

Section 66. Law Granting Donation or Gratuity

Section 67. Time Limit for Introducing New Bill

Section 68. Precedence and Time Limits for Appropriation and Revenue Bills

Section 69. Contents of Appropriation Bills

Section 70. Votes Required for Passage of Revenue or Property Assessment Bills

Section 71. Title of Bill; Committee Recommendations

Section 72. Approval or Disapproval of Bill by Governor; Veto Override Process

Section 73. Veto of Parts of Appropriations Bill

Section 74. Referral of Bill to Committee

Section 75. Enforcement of Laws of General Nature

Section 76. Viva Voce Vote

Section 77. Writs of Election to Fill Legislative Vacancies

INJUNCTIONS

Section 78. Salary Deductions for Neglect of Official Duty

Section 79. Sale of Delinquent Tax Lands; Right of Redemption

Section 80. Abuse of Certain Local Government Unit Powers

Section 81. Obstruction of Navigable Waters; Certain Construction Projects Authorized

Section 82. Official Bonds; Fixing Penalties

Section 83. Fire Safety in Certain Public Places

Section 84. Acquisition of Land by Nonresident Aliens and Corporations

Section 85. Working of Public Roads by Contract or by County Prisoners

Section 86. Care of Insane and Indigent Sick

LOCAL LEGISLATION PROHIBITIONS

Section 87. Special or Local Laws

Section 88. Content of General Laws

Section 89. Standing Committee for Local and Private Legislation in Each House

Section 90. Matters Provided for by General Laws Only

PROHIBITIONS

Section 91. Uniform Application of Charges and Fees

Section 92. Salary of Deceased Officer

Section 93. Retirement of Officer On Pay

Section 94. Disability On Account of Coverture Abolished

Section 95. Donation or Sale of State Lands; Railroad Easements

Section 96. Extra Compensation and Unauthorized Payments Prohibited

Section 97. Revival of Action Barred by Limitations Prohibited

Section 98. Repealed

Section 99. Election of Officers by Legislature

Section 100. Release of Obligation or Liability Owed to State or Political Subdivision

Section 101. Seat of State Government

MISCELLANEOUS

Section 102. Elections for State and County Officers

Section 103. Filling Public Officer Vacancies; Compensation and Powers of Officers

Section 104. Statutes of Limitation Not to Run Against State and Political Subdivisions

Section 105. Repealed

Section 106. State Librarian

Section 107. Bidding and Other Requirements for Certain Contracts

Section 108. Termination of Duties Pertaining to Office

Section 109. Interest of Public Officer in Contracts

Section 110. Rights of Way for Private Roads

Section 111. Sale of Land by Decree or Execution

Section 112. Equal Taxation; Property Tax Assessments

Section 113. Auditor's Statement of Money Expended at Session

Section 114. Election Returns

Section 115. Fiscal Year; Report of Transactions; Bonded Indebtedness Limitation

Article V: Executive – Page 64

Section 116. Governor; Term of Office

Section 117. Eligibility to Serve as Governor

Section 118. Salary of Governor

Section 119. Commander-in-Chief of Military

Section 120. Report From Officers of Executive Department

Section 121. Convening of Legislature in Extraordinary Session

Section 122. State of The Government; Recommending Measures

Section 123. Faithful Execution of Laws

Section 124. Reprieves and Pardons

Section 125. Suspension of Defaulting Treasurers and Tax Collectors

Section 126. Seal of State

Section 127. Commissions

Section 128. Lieutenant Governor; Qualifications and Term

Section 129. Lieutenant Governor as President of Senate

Section 130. Salary of Lieutenant Governor

Section 131. Vacancy in Office of Governor

Section 132. Contested Election for Lieutenant Governor

Section 133. Secretary of State

Section 134. State Treasurer; Auditor of Public Accounts

Section 135. County Officers

Section 136. Continuation in Office

Section 137. Repealed

Section 138. Selection of County Officers

Section 139. Removal and Appointment of County and Municipal Officers

Section 140. Election of Governor

Section 141. Choosing Governor in Absence of Electoral and Popular Vote Majorities

Section 142. Ineligibility of Legislators to Receive Certain Appointments

Section 143. Election of Other State Officers

Article VI: Judiciary – Page 72

Section 144. Judicial Power of State

Section 145. Composition of Supreme Court

Section 145-A. Addition of Judges to Supreme Court

Section 145-B. Further Addition of Judges to Supreme Court

Section 146. Jurisdiction of Supreme Court

Section 147. Reversal of Judgment for Want of Jurisdiction; Remand

Section 148. Holding of Supreme Court at Seat of Government

Section 149. Term of Office of Supreme Court Judges

Section 149-A. Divisions of Supreme Court

Section 150. Eligibility Requirements for Supreme Court Judges

Section 151. Repealed

Section 152. Circuit and Chancery Court Districts

Section 153. Election and Terms of Circuit and Chancery Court Judges

Section 154. Qualifications for Circuit or Chancery Court Judges

Section 155. Judicial Oath of Office

Section 156. Jurisdiction of Circuit Court

Section 157. Exclusive Jurisdiction of Chancery Court; Transfer

Section 158. Holding of Circuit Court

Section 159. Jurisdiction of Chancery Court

Section 160. Additional Jurisdiction of Chancery Court

Section 161. Concurrent Jurisdiction of Chancery and Circuit Court

Section 162. Transfer to Circuit Court

Section 163. Certification of Transferred Causes

Section 164. Holding of Chancery Court

Section 165. Disqualification of Judges

Section 166. Compensation of Judges

Section 167. Civil Officers as Conservators of Peace

Section 168. Clerks of Court

Section 169. Style of Process

Section 170. County Districts; Board of Supervisors

Section 171. Justice Court Judges; Jurisdiction

Section 172. Establishment and Abolishment of Inferior Courts

Section 172-A. Court Order for Tax Levy or Tax Increase Prohibited

Section 173. Attorney General

Section 174. District Attorneys

Section 175. Liability and Punishment of Public Officers

Section 176. Qualifications for Member of Board of Supervisors

Section 177. Vacancy in Office of Judge or Chancellor

Section 177-A. Commission On Judicial Performance

Article VII: Corporations – Page 85

Section 178. Formation; Charter of Incorporation

Section 179. Compliance With Provisions

Section 180. Organization

Section 181. Taxation

Section 182. Tax Exemptions

Section 183. Subscription to Capital Stock by Counties or Municipalities

Section 184. Railroads

Section 185. Rolling-Stock as Personal Property Subject to Execution and Sale

Section 186. Telephone, Telegraph and Railroad Charges

Section 187. Repealed

Section 188. Free or Discounted Tickets to Public Officers

Section 189. Repealed

Section 190. Eminent Domain; Police Powers

Section 191. Protection of Corporate Employees

Section 192. Public Utilities May Be Exempted From Municipal Tax; Duration

Section 193. Remedy for Injury to Railroad Employee

Section 194. Repealed

Section 195. Common Carriers Designated

Section 196. Repealed

Section 197. Repealed

Section 198. Trusts, Combinations, Contracts and Agreements Inimical to Public Welfare

Section 198-A. Right to Work; Labor Unions

Section 199. "Corporation" Defined

Section 200. Enforcement of Provisions

Article VIII: Education – Page 93

Section 201. Free Public Schools

Section 202. State Superintendent of Public Education

Section 203. State Board of Education

Section 204. County Superintendents of Education

Section 205. Repealed

Section 206. State Common-School Fund; Additional Tax Levy by District

Section 206-A. Establishment of Education Improvement Trust Fund

Section 207. Repealed

Section 208. Control of Funds by Religious Sect; Certain Appropriations Prohibited

Section 209. Institutions for Education of Deaf, Dumb and Blind

Section 210. Sale of Public School Supplies

Section 211. Sixteenth Section Lands

Section 212. Interest Rate On Chickasaw School Fund and Other Educational Trust Funds

Section 213. Agricultural and Mechanical Colleges

Section 213-A. State Institutions of Higher Learning

Section 213-B. Repealed

Section 201. Free Public Schools

Article IX: Militia – Page 103

Section 214. Persons Subject to Military Duty

Section 215. Organization of Militia by Legislature

Section 216. Appointment and Removal of Militia Officers

Section 217. Governor as Commander-in-Chief

Section 218. Major-General; Brigadier-General

Section 219. Adjutant-General

Section 220. Exemption of Militia From Arrest for Certain Offenses

Section 221. Appropriations for Mississippi National Guard

Section 222. Support of Mississippi National Guard by County Boards of Supervisors

Article X: The Penitentiary and Prisons – Page 106

Section 223. Repealed

Section 224. Employment of Convicts On Public Roads, Public Works or Public Levee Projects

Section 225. Placement of Convicts On State Farms; Prison. Industries; Reformatory Schools; Good Behavior

Section 226. Hire or Lease of County Jail Inmates

Article XI: Levees – Page 106

Section 227. Maintenance of Levee System

Section 228. Levee Districts

Section 229. Boards of Levee Commissioners

Section 230. Commissioner Qualifications and Bond

Section 231. Election of Commissioners

Section 232. Duties and Powers of Commissioners

Section 233. Appropriation of Private Property

Section 234. Bills Changing District Boundaries or Taxes

Section 235. Report by Levee Board

Section 236. Levee Taxes

Section 237. System of Levee Taxation

Section 238. Property Exempt From Levee Taxation

Section 239. Publication of Itemized Account

Article XII: Franchise – Page 111

Section 240. Elections to Be by Ballot

Section 241. Qualifications for Electors

Section 241-A. Repealed

Section 242. Voter Registration

Section 243. Repealed

Section 244. Repealed

Section 244-A. Additional Qualifications for Voter Registration

Section 245. Elector Qualifications in Municipal Elections

Section 246. Regulation of Elections

Section 247. Securing Fairness in Party Primary Elections and Conventions

Section 248. Remedies for Illegal or Improper Registration

Section 249. Registration Required to Vote

Section 249-A. Government Issued Photo Identification Required to Vote

Section 250. Qualified Electors Eligible for Office

Section 251. Time of Registration

Section 252. Terms of Office; General Election Dates

Section 253. Restoration of Right of Suffrage After Crime

Article XIII: Apportionment – Page 116

Section 254. Senatorial and Representative Districts

Section 255. Repealed

Section 256. Repealed

Article XIV: General Provision – Page 117

Section 257. Commencement of Political Year

Section 258. Credit of State

Section 259. Removal of County Seat

Section 260. Formation of New County; Changing Judicial Districts

Section 261. Expenses of Criminal Prosecutions; Fines, Forfeitures and Costs

Section 262. Asylums for The Aged or Infirm

Section 263. Repealed

Section 263-A. Marriage Defined as Only Between A Man and A Woman

Section 264. Qualifications of Grand and Petit Jurors

Section 265. Denial of Supreme Being Disqualification to Hold Office

Section 266. Holding Office Under Federal or Foreign Government

Section 267. Devotion of Time to Office

Section 268. Oath of Office

Section 269. Repealed

Section 270. Repealed

Section 271. Consolidation of Counties

Section 272. Repealed

Section 272-A. Retirement Systems

Article XV: Amendments to the Constitution – Page 121

In General:

Amendments

Section 273. Amendment Process

Schedule – Page 127

Section 274. Laws to Remain in Force

Section 275. Repeal of Laws Repugnant to Constitution

Section 276. Laws Repugnant to Franchise and Election Provisions

Section 277. Laws Repugnant to Apportionment Provisions

Section 278. Appointment of Persons to Draft Laws

Section 279. Continuation of Writs, Actions and Causes of Action

Section 280. Jurisdiction of Courts in Preexisting Actions

Section 281. Accrual of Fines, Penalties and Forfeitures

Section 282. Preexisting Bonds Remain Binding

Section 283. Crimes and Misdemeanors

Section 284. Continuation in Office

Section 285. Abrogated or Repealed Laws Not Revived

Sections 286 and 287. Renumbered

PREAMBLE

We, the people of Mississippi in convention assembled, grateful to Almighty God, and invoking his blessing on our work, do ordain and establish this constitution.

ARTICLE I: DISTRIBUTION OF POWERS

Section 1. Powers of Government

The powers of the government of the State of Mississippi shall be divided into three distinct departments, and each of them confided to a separate magistracy, to-wit: those which are legislative to one, those which are judicial to another, and those which are executive to another.

Section 2. Encroachment of Power

No person or collection of persons, being one or belonging to one of these departments, shall exercise any power properly belonging to either of the others. The acceptance of an office in either of said departments shall, of itself, and at once, vacate any and all offices held by the person so accepting in either of the other departments.

ARTICLE II: BOUNDARIES OF THE STATE SECTION

Section 3. Repealed

Section 4. Acquisition of Territory; Disputed Boundaries

The Legislature shall have power to consent to the acquisition of additional territory by the state, and to make the same a part thereof; and the Legislature may settle disputed boundaries between this state and its coterminus states whenever such disputes arise.

ARTICLE III: BILL OF RIGHTS

Section 5. Government Originating in The People

All political power is vested in, and derived from, the people; all government of right originates with the people, is founded upon their will only, and is instituted solely for the good of the whole.

Section 6. Regulation of Government; Right to Alter

The people of this state have the inherent, sole, and exclusive right to regulate the internal government and police thereof, and to alter and abolish their constitution and form of government whenever they deem it necessary to their safety and happiness; Provided, Such change be not repugnant to the constitution of the United States.

Section 7. Secession Prohibited

The right to withdraw from the Federal Union on account of any real or supposed grievance, shall never be assumed by this state, nor shall any law be passed in derogation of the paramount allegiance of the citizens of this state to the government of the United States.

Section 8. Citizens of State

All persons, resident in this State, citizens of the United States, are hereby declared citizens of the State of Mississippi.

Section 9. Subordination of Military to Civil Power

The military shall be in strict subordination to the civil power.

Section 10. Treason

Treason against the state shall consist only in levying war against the same or in adhering to its enemies, giving them aid and comfort. No person shall be convicted of treason unless on the testimony of two witnesses to the same overt act, or on confession in open court.

Section 11. Peaceful Assemblage; Right to Petition Government

The right of the people peaceably to assemble and petition the government on any subject shall never be impaired.

Section 12. Right to Bear Arms

The right of every citizen to keep and bear arms in defense of his home, person, or property, or in aid of the civil power when thereto legally summoned, shall not be called in question, but the Legislature may regulate or forbid carrying concealed weapons.

Section 13. Freedom of Speech and Press; Libel

The freedom of speech and of the press shall be held sacred; and in all prosecutions for libel the truth may be given in evidence, and the jury shall determine the law and the facts under the direction of the court; and if it shall appear to the jury that the matter charged as libelous is true, and was published with good motives and for justifiable ends, the party shall be acquitted.

Section 14. Due Process

No person shall be deprived of life, liberty, or property except by due process of law.

Section 15. Slavery and Involuntary Servitude Prohibited; Punishment for Crime

There shall be neither slavery nor involuntary servitude in this state, otherwise than in the punishment of crime, whereof the party shall have been duly convicted.

Section 16. Ex Post Facto Laws; Impairment of Contract

Ex post facto laws, or laws impairing the obligation of contracts, shall not be passed.

Section 17. Taking Property for Public Use; Due Compensation

Private property shall not be taken or damaged for public use, except on due compensation being first made to the owner or owners thereof, in a manner to be prescribed by law; and whenever an attempt is made to take private property for a use alleged to be public, the question whether the contemplated use be public shall be a judicial question, and, as such, determined

Section 17-A. Taking Private Property by Eminent Domain; Transfer to Others Prohibited for Ten (10) Years; Exceptions

No property acquired by the exercise of the power of eminent domain under the laws of the State of Mississippi shall, for a period of ten years after its acquisition, be transferred or any interest therein transferred to any person, non-governmental entity, public-private partnership, corporation, or other business entity with the following exceptions:

(1) The above provisions shall not apply to drainage and levee facilities and usage, roads and bridges for public conveyance, flood control projects with a levee component, seawalls, dams, toll roads, public airports, public ports, public harbors, public wayports, common carriers or facilities for public utilities and other entities used in the generation, transmission, storage or distribution of telephone, telecommunication, gas carbon dioxide, electricity, water, sewer, natural gas, liquid hydrocarbons or other utility products.

(2) The above provisions shall not apply where the use of eminent domain

(a) removes a public nuisance;

(b) removes a structure that is beyond repair or unfit for human habitation or use;

(c) is used to acquire abandoned property; or

(d) eliminates a direct threat to public health or safety caused by the property in its current condition.

Section 18. Freedom of Religion

No religious test as a qualification for office shall be required; and no preference shall be given by law to any religious sect or mode of worship; but the free enjoyment of all religious sentiments and the different modes of worship shall be held sacred. The rights hereby secured shall not be construed to justify acts of licentiousness injurious to morals or dangerous to the peace and safety of the state, or to exclude the Holy Bible from use in any public school of this state.

Section 19. Repealed

Section 20. Specific Term of Office

No person shall be elected or appointed to office in this state for life or during good behavior, but the term of all officers shall be for some specified period.

Section 21. Writ of Habeas Corpus

The privilege of the writ of habeas corpus shall not be suspended, unless when in the case of rebellion or invasion, the public safety may require it, nor ever without the authority of the legislature.

Section 22. Double Jeopardy

No person's life or liberty shall be twice placed in jeopardy for the same offense; but there must be an actual acquittal or conviction on the merits to bar another prosecution.

Section 23. Searches and Seizures

The people shall be secure in their persons, houses, and possessions, from unreasonable seizure or search; and no warrant shall be issued without probable cause, supported by oath or affirmation, specially designating the place to be searched and the person or thing to be seized.

Section 24. Open Courts; Remedy for Injury

All courts shall be open; and every person for an injury done him in his lands, goods, person, or reputation, shall have remedy by due course of law, and right and justice shall be administered without sale, denial, or delay.

Section 25. Access to Courts

No person shall be debarred from prosecuting or defending any civil cause for or against him or herself, before any tribunal in the state, by him or herself, or counsel, or both.

Section 26. Rights of Accused; State Grand Jury Proceedings

In all criminal prosecutions the accused shall have a right to be heard by himself or counsel, or both, to demand the nature and cause of the accusation, to be confronted by the witnesses against him, to have compulsory process for obtaining witnesses in his favor, and, in all prosecutions by indictment or information, a speedy and public trial by an impartial jury of the county where the offense was committed; and he shall not be compelled to give evidence against himself; but in prosecutions for rape, adultery, fornication, sodomy or crime against nature the court may, in its discretion, exclude from the courtroom all persons except such as are necessary in the conduct of the trial. Notwithstanding any other provisions of this Constitution, the Legislature may enact laws establishing a state grand jury with the authority to return indictments regardless of the county where the crime was committed. The subject matter jurisdiction of a state grand jury is limited to criminal violations of the Mississippi Uniform Controlled Substances Law or any other crime involving narcotics, dangerous drugs or controlled substances, or any crime arising out of or in connection with a violation of the Mississippi Uniform Controlled Substances Law or a crime involving narcotics, dangerous drugs or controlled substances if the crime occurs within more than one (1) circuit court district of the state or transpires or has significance in more than one (1) circuit court district of the state. The venue for the trial of indictments returned by a state grand jury shall be as prescribed by general law.

Section 26-A. Victims Rights; Construction of Provisions; Legislative Authority

(1) Victims of crime, as defined by law, shall have the right to be treated with fairness, dignity and respect throughout the criminal justice process; and to be informed, to be present and to be heard, when authorized by law, during public hearings.

(2) Nothing in this section shall provide grounds for the accused or convicted offender to obtain any form of relief nor shall this section impair the constitutional rights of the accused. Nothing in this section or any enabling statute shall be construed as creating a cause of action for damages against the state or any of its agencies, officials, employees or political subdivisions.

(3) The Legislature shall have the authority to enact substantive and procedural laws to define, implement, preserve and protect the rights guaranteed to victims by this section.

Section 27. Proceeding by Indictment or Information

No person shall, for any indictable offense, be proceeded against criminally by information, except in cases arising in the land or naval forces, or the military when in actual service, or by leave of the court for misdemeanor in office or where a defendant represented by counsel by sworn statement waives indictment; but the legislature, in cases not punishable by death or by imprisonment in the penitentiary, may dispense with the inquest of the grand jury, and may authorize prosecutions before justice court judges, or such other inferior court or courts as may be established, and the proceedings in such cases shall be regulated by law.

Section 28. Cruel or Unusual Punishment Prohibited

Cruel or unusual punishment shall not be inflicted, nor excessive fines be imposed.

Section 29. Excessive Bail Prohibited; Revocation or Denial of Bail

(1) Excessive bail shall not be required, and all persons shall, before conviction, be bailable by sufficient sureties, except for capital offenses

(a) when the proof is evident or presumption great; or

(b) when the person has previously been convicted of a capital offense or any other offense punishable by imprisonment for a maximum of twenty (20) years or more.

(2) If a person charged with committing any offense that is punishable by death, life imprisonment or imprisonment for one (1) year or more in the penitentiary or any other state correctional facility is granted bail and

(a) if that person is indicted for a felony committed while on bail; or

(b) if the court, upon hearing, finds probable cause that the person has committed a felony while on bail, then the court shall revoke bail and shall order that the person be detained, without further bail, pending trial of the charge for which bail was revoked. for the purposes of this subsection (2) only, the term "felony" means any offense punishable by death, life imprisonment or imprisonment for more than five (5) years under the laws of the jurisdiction in which the crime is committed. In addition, grand larceny shall be considered a felony for the purposes of this subsection.

(3) In the case of offenses punishable by imprisonment for a maximum of twenty (20) years or more or by life imprisonment, a county or circuit court judge may deny bail for such offenses when the proof is evident or the presumption great upon making a determination that the release of the person or persons arrested for such offense would constitute a special danger to any other person or to the community or that no condition or combination of conditions will reasonably assure the appearance of the person as required.

(4) In any case where bail is denied before conviction, the judge shall place in the record his reasons for denying bail. Any person who is charged with an offense punishable by imprisonment for a maximum of twenty (20) years or more or by life imprisonment and who is denied bail prior to conviction shall be entitled to an emergency hearing before a justice of the Mississippi Supreme Court. The provisions of this subsection (4) do not apply to bail revocation orders.

Section 30. Imprisonment for Debt

There shall be no imprisonment for debt.

Section 31. Trial by Jury

The right of trial by jury shall remain inviolate, but the Legislature may, by enactment, provide that in all civil suits tried in the circuit and chancery court, nine or more jurors may agree on the verdict and return it as the verdict of the jury.

Section 32. Construction of Enumerated Rights

The enumeration of rights in this constitution shall not be construed to deny and impair others retained by, and inherent in, the people.

ARTICLE IV: LEGISLATIVE DEPARTMENT

IN GENERAL

Section 33. Composition of Legislature

The legislative power of this state shall be vested in a Legislature which shall consist of a Senate and a House of Representatives.

Section 34. Composition of House of Representatives

The House of Representatives shall consist of members chosen every four years by the qualified electors of the several counties and Representative districts.

Section 35. Composition of Senate

The Senate shall consist of members chosen every four years by the qualified electors of the several districts.

Section 36. Sessions

The Legislature shall meet at the seat of government in regular session on the Tuesday after the first Monday of January of the year A.D., 1970, and annually thereafter, unless sooner convened by the Governor; provided, however, that such sessions shall be limited to a period of one hundred twenty-five (125) calendar days for regular 1972 session and every fourth year thereafter, but ninety (90) calendar days for every other regular session thereafter. Provided further that the House of Representatives, by resolution with the Senate concurring therein, and by a two-thirds (2/3) vote of those present and voting in each house, may extend such limited session for a period of thirty (30) days with no limit on the number of extensions to each session.

Section 37. Elections for Members

Elections for members of the Legislature shall be held in the several counties and districts as provided by law.

Section 38. Election of Officers by Each House

Each house shall elect its own officers, and shall judge of the qualifications, return and election of its own members.

Section 39. President Pro Tempore of Senate

The Senate shall choose a President pro tempore to act in the absence or disability of its presiding officer.

QUALIFICATIONS AND PRIVILEGES OF LEGISLATORS

Section 40. Oath of Office

Members of the Legislature, before entering upon the discharge of their duties, shall take the following oath: "I, _____ , do solemnly swear (or affirm) that I will faithfully support the Constitution of the United States and of the State of Mississippi; that I am not disqualified from holding office by the Constitution of this state; that I will faithfully discharge my duties as a legislator; that I will, as soon as practicable hereafter, carefully read (or have read to me) the Constitution of this State, and will endeavor to note, and as a legislator to execute, all the requirements thereof imposed on the Legislature; and I will not vote for any measure or person because of a promise of any other member of this Legislature to vote for any measure or person, or as a means of influencing him or them so to do. So help me God."

Section 41. Qualifications of House of Representatives Members

No person shall be a member of the House of Representatives who shall not have attained the age of twenty-one (21) years, and who shall not be a qualified elector of the State, and who shall not have been a resident citizen of the State for four (4) years, and within the district such person seeks to serve for two (2) years, immediately preceding his election. The seat of a member of the House of Representatives shall be vacated on his removal from the district from which he was elected.

Section 42. Qualifications of Senators

No person shall be a Senator who shall not have attained the age of twenty-five years, who shall not have been a qualified elector of the State four years, and who shall not be an actual resident of the district or territory he may be chosen to represent for two years before his election. The seat of a Senator shall be vacated upon his removal from the district from which he was elected.

Section 43. Person Liable for Public Monies Ineligible for Office

No person liable as principal for public moneys unaccounted for shall be eligible to a seat in either house of the legislature, or to any office of profit or trust, until he shall have accounted for and paid over all sums for which he may have been liable.

Section 44. Ineligibility for Office of Person Convicted of Certain Crimes

(1) No person shall be eligible to a seat in either House of the Legislature, or to any office of profit or trust, who shall have been convicted of bribery, perjury, or other infamous crime; and any person who shall have been convicted of giving or offering, directly, or indirectly, any bribe to procure his election or appointment, and any person who shall give or offer any bribe to procure the election or appointment of any person to office, shall, on conviction thereof, be disqualified from holding any office of profit or trust under the laws of this state.

(2) No person who is convicted after ratification of this amendment in another state of any offense which is a felony under the laws of this state, and no person who is convicted after ratification of this amendment of any felony in a federal court, shall be eligible to hold any office of profit or trust in this state.

(3) This section shall not disqualify a person from holding office if he has been pardoned for the offense or if the offense of which the person was convicted was manslaughter, any violation of the United States Internal Revenue Code or any violation of the tax laws of this state unless such offense also involved misuse or abuse of his office or money coming into his hands by virtue of his office.

Section 45. Member Eligibility for Offices Created During Term of Office

No Senator or Representative, during the term for which he was elected, shall be eligible to any office of profit which shall have been created, or the emoluments of which have been increased, during the time such Senator or Representative was in office, except to such offices as may be filled by an election of the people.

Section 46. Salaries of Members

The members of the Legislature shall severally receive from the State Treasury compensation for their services, to be prescribed by law, which may be increased or diminished; but no alteration of such compensation of members shall take effect during the session at which it is made.

Section 47. Fees or Rewards Prohibited

No member of the Legislature shall take any fee or reward, or be counsel in any measure pending before either house of the legislature, under penalty of forfeiting his seat, upon proof thereof to the satisfaction of the house of which he is a member.

Section 48. Immunity of Members From Arrest for Certain Crimes

Senators and Representatives shall, in all cases, except treason, felony, theft, or breach of the peace, be privileged from arrest during the session of the Legislature, and for fifteen days before the commencement and after the termination of each session.

Section 49. Power of Impeachment

The House of Representatives shall have the sole power of impeachment; but two-thirds of all the members present must concur therein. All impeachments shall be tried by the Senate, and, when sitting for that purpose, the Senators shall be sworn to do justice according to law and the evidence.

Section 50. Impeachment Grounds

The Governor and all other civil officers of this State, shall be liable to impeachment for treason, bribery, or any high crime or misdemeanor in office.

Section 51. Removal From Office

Judgment in such cases shall not extend further than removal from office and disqualification to hold any office of honor, trust, or profit in this State; but the party convicted shall, nevertheless, be subject to indictment, trial, judgment, and punishment according to law.

Section 52. Persons to Preside in Impeachment Proceedings

When the Governor shall be tried, the Chief Justice of the Supreme Court shall preside; and when the Chief Justice is disabled, disqualified, or refuses to act, the judge of the Supreme Court next oldest in commission shall preside; and no person shall be convicted without concurrence of two-thirds of all the Senators present.

Section 53. Removal of Judges for Reasonable Cause

for reasonable cause, which shall not be sufficient ground of impeachment, the Governor shall, on the joint address of two-thirds of each branch of the Legislature, remove from office the judges of the Supreme and inferior courts; but the cause or causes of removal shall be spread on the journal, and the party charged be notified of the same, and have an opportunity to be heard by himself or counsel, or both, before the vote is finally taken and decided.

RULES OF PROCEDURE

Section 54. Quorum

A majority of each House shall constitute a quorum to do business; but a less number may adjourn from day to day, and compel the attendance of absent members in such manner and under such penalties as each shall provide.

Section 55. Determination of Rules by Each House

Each House may determine rules of its own proceedings, punish its members for disorderly behavior, and, with the concurrence of two-thirds of the members present, expel a member; but no member, unless expelled for theft, bribery, or corruption, shall be expelled the second time for the same offense. Both houses shall, from time to time, publish journals of their proceedings, except such parts as may, in their opinion, require secrecy; and the yeas and nays, on any question, shall be entered on the journal, at the request of one-tenth of the members present; and the yeas and nays shall be entered on the journals on the final passage of every bill.

Section 56. Style of Laws

The style of the laws of the State shall be: "Be it enacted by the Legislature of the state of Mississippi."

57. Adjournments; Meeting Place

Neither House shall, without the consent of the other, adjourn for more than three days, nor to any other place than that in which the two houses shall be sitting.

Section 58. Open Door Policy; Disorderly Behavior

The doors of each House, when in session, or in committee of the whole, shall be kept open, except in cases which may require secrecy; and each House may punish, by fine and imprisonment, any person not a member who shall be guilty of disrespect to the House by any disorderly or contemptuous behavior in its presence, or who shall in any way disturb its deliberations during the session; but such imprisonment shall not extend beyond the final adjournment of that session.

Section 59. Introduction and Passage of Bills

Bills may originate in either House, and be amended or rejected in the other, and every bill shall be read by its title on three (3) different days in each House, unless two-thirds (2/3) of the house where the same is pending shall dispense with the rules; and every bill shall be read in full immediately before the vote on its final passage upon the demand of any member; and every bill, having passed both Houses, shall be signed by the President of the Senate and the Speaker of the House of Representatives during the legislative session.

Section 60. Amendment of Bill; Orders, Votes and Resolutions

No bill shall be so amended in its passage through either house as to change its original purpose, and no law shall be passed except by bill; but orders, votes, and resolutions of both houses, affecting the prerogatives and duties thereof, or relating to adjournment, to amendments to the Constitution, to the investigation of public officers, and the like, shall not require the signature of the governor; and such resolutions, orders, and votes, may empower legislative committees to administer oaths, to send for persons and papers, and generally make legislative investigations effective.

Section 61. Amendment or Revival by Reference to Title Prohibited

No law shall be revived or amended by reference to its title only, but the section or sections, as amended or revived, shall be inserted at length.

Section 62. Voting On Amendments; Adoption of Committee Reports

No amendment to bills by one House shall be concurred in by the other except by a vote of the majority thereof, taken by yeas and nays and the names of those voting for and against recorded upon the journals; and reports of committees of conference shall in like manner be adopted in each house.

Section 63. Maximum Sum Fixed in Appropriation Bill

No appropriation bill shall be passed by the Legislature which does not fix definitely the maximum sum thereby authorized to be drawn from the treasury.

Section 64. Time Limit and Voting Requirements for Appropriations

No bill passed after the adoption of this Constitution to make appropriations of money out of the State Treasury shall continue in force more than two months after the expiration of the fiscal year ending after the meeting of the Legislature at its next regular session; nor shall such bill be passed except by the votes of a majority of all members elected to each House of the

Legislature.

Section 65. Reconsideration of Votes

All votes on the final passage of any measure shall be subject to reconsideration for at least one whole legislative day, and no motion to reconsider such vote shall be disposed of adversely on the day on which the original vote was taken, except on the last day of the session.

Section 66. Law Granting Donation or Gratuity

No law granting a donation or gratuity in favor of any person or object shall be enacted except by the concurrence of two-thirds of the members elect of each branch of the Legislature, nor by any vote for a sectarian purpose or use.

Section 67. Time Limit for Introducing New Bill

No new bill shall be introduced into either House of the Legislature during the last three days of the session.

Section 68. Precedence and Time Limits for Appropriation and Revenue Bills

Appropriation and revenue bills shall, at regular sessions of the Legislature, have precedence in both houses over all other business, and no such bills shall be passed during the last five days of the session.

Section 69. Contents of Appropriation Bills

General appropriation bills shall contain only the appropriations to defray the ordinary expenses of the executive, legislative, and judicial departments of the government; to pay interest on state bonds, and to support the common schools. All other appropriations shall be made by separate bills, each embracing but one subject. Legislation shall not be engrafted on the appropriation bills, but the same may prescribe the conditions on which the money may be drawn, and for what purposes paid.

Section 70. Votes Required for Passage of Revenue or Property Assessment Bills

No revenue bill, or any bill providing for assessments of property for taxation, shall become a law except by a vote of at least three-fifths of the members of each house present and voting.

Section 71. Title of Bill; Committee Recommendations

Every bill introduced into the Legislature shall have a title, and the title ought to indicate clearly the subject matter or matters of the proposed legislation. Each committee to which a bill may be referred shall express, in writing, its judgment of the sufficiency of the title of the bill, and this, too, whether the recommendation be that the bill do pass or do not pass.

Section 72. Approval or Disapproval of Bill by Overnor; Veto Override Process

Every Bill which shall pass both Houses shall be presented to the Governor of the state. If he approve, he shall sign it; but if he does not approve, he shall return it, with his objections, to the House in which it originated, which shall enter the objections at large upon its Journal, and proceed to reconsider it. If after such reconsideration two-thirds (2/3) of that House shall agree to pass the Bill, it shall be sent, with the objections, to the other House, by which, likewise, it shall be reconsidered; and if approved by two-thirds (2/3) of that House, it shall become a law; but in all such cases the votes of both Houses shall be determined by yeas and nays, and the names of the persons voting for and against the Bill shall be entered on the Journal of each House respectively. If any Bill shall not be returned by the Governor within five (5) days (Sundays excepted) after it has been presented to him, it shall become a law in like manner as if he had signed it, unless the Legislature, by adjournment, prevented its return, in which case such Bill shall be a law unless the Governor shall veto it within fifteen (15) days (Sundays excepted) after it is presented to him, and such Bill shall be returned to the Legislature, with his objections, within three (3) days after the beginning of the next session of the Legislature.

Section 73. Veto of Parts of Appropriations Bill

The Governor may veto parts of any appropriation bill, and approve parts of the same, and the portions approved shall be law.

Section 74. Referral of Bill to Committee

No bill shall become a law until it shall have been referred to a committee of each House and returned therefrom with a recommendation in writing.

Section 75. Enforcement of Laws of General Nature

No law of a general nature, unless therein otherwise provided, shall be enforced until sixty days after its passage.

Section 76. Viva Voce Vote

In all elections by the Legislature the members shall vote viva voce, and the vote shall be entered on the journals.

Section 77. Writs of Election to Fill Legislative Vacancies

The Governor shall issue writs of election to fill such vacancies as may occur in either house of the legislature, and the persons thereupon chosen shall hold their seats for the unexpired term.

INJUNCTIONS

Section 78. Salary Deductions for Neglect of Official Duty

It shall be the duty of the Legislature to regulate by law the cases in which deductions shall be made from salaries of public officers for neglect of official duty, and the amount of said deduction.

Section 79. Sale of Delinquent Tax Lands; Right of Redemption

The Legislature shall provide by law for the sale of all delinquent tax lands. The courts shall apply the same liberal principles in favor of such titles as in sale by execution. The right of redemption from all sales of real estate, for the nonpayment of taxes or special assessments, of any and every character whatsoever, shall exist, on conditions to be prescribed by law, in favor of owners and persons interested in such real estate, for a period of not less than two years.

Section 80. Abuse of Certain Local Government Unit Powers

Provision shall be made by general laws to prevent the abuse by cities, towns, and other municipal corporations of their powers of assessment, taxation, borrowing money, and contracting debts.

Section 81. Obstruction of Navigable Waters; Certain Construction Projects Authorized

The Legislature shall never authorize the permanent obstruction of any of the navigable waters of the State, but may provide for the removal of such obstructions as now exist, whenever the public welfare demands. This section shall not prevent the construction, under proper authority, of drawbridges for railroads, or other roads, nor the construction of booms and chutes for logs, nor the construction, operation and maintenance of facilities incident to the exploration, production or transportation of oil, gas or other minerals, nor the construction, operation and maintenance of bridges and causeways in such manner as not to prevent the safe passage of vessels or logs under regulations to be provided by law.

Section 82. Official Bonds; Fixing Penalties

The Legislature shall fix the amount of the penalty of all official bonds, and may, as far as practicable, provide that the whole or a part of the security required for the faithful discharge of official duty shall be made by some guarantee company or companies. SECTION 83. Fire safety in certain public places. The Legislature shall enact laws to secure the safety of persons from fires in hotels, theaters, and other public places of resort.

Section 84. Acquisition of Land by Nonresident Aliens and Corporations

The Legislature shall enact laws to limit, restrict, or prevent the acquiring and holding of land in this State by nonresident aliens, and may limit or restrict the acquiring or holding of lands by corporations.

Section 85. Working of Public Roads by Contract or by County Prisoners

The Legislature shall provide by general law for the working of public roads by contract or by county prisoners, or both. Such law may be put in operation only by a vote of the board of supervisors in those counties where it may be desirable.

SECTION 86. Care of insane and indigent sick

It shall be the duty of the Legislature to provide by law for the treatment and care of the insane; and the Legislature may provide for the care of the indigent sick in the hospitals in the State.

LOCAL LEGISLATION

Section 87. Special or Local Laws

No special or local law shall be enacted for the benefit of individuals or corporations, in cases which are or can be provided for by general law, or where the relief sought can be given by any court of this State; nor shall the operation of any general law be suspended by the Legislature for the benefit of any individual or private corporation or association, and in all cases where a general law can be made applicable, and would be advantageous, no special law shall be enacted.

Section 88. Content of General Laws

The Legislature shall pass general laws, under which local and private interest shall be provided for and protected, and under which cities and towns may be chartered and their charters amended, and under which corporations may be created, organized, and their acts of incorporation altered; and all such laws shall be subject to repeal or amendment.

Section 89. Standing Committee for Local and Private Legislation in Each House

There shall be appointed in each house of the Legislature a standing committee on local and private legislation; the house committee to consist of seven Representatives, and the Senate committee of five Senators. No local or private bill shall be passed by either House until it shall have been referred to said committee thereof, and shall have been reported back with a recommendation in writing that it do pass, stating affirmatively the reasons therefor, and why the end to be accomplished should not be reached by a general law, or by a proceeding in court; or if the recommendation of the committee be that the bill do not pass, then it shall not pass the House to which it is so reported unless it be voted for by a majority of all members elected thereto. If a bill is passed in conformity to the requirements hereof, other than such as are prohibited in the next section, the courts shall not, because of its local, special, or private nature, refuse to enforce it.

Section 90. Matters Provided for by General Laws Only

The Legislature shall not pass local, private, or special laws in any of the following enumerated cases, but such matters shall be provided for only by general laws, viz.:

(a) Granting divorces;

(b) Changing the names of persons, places, or corporations;

(c) Providing for changes of venue in civil and criminal cases;

(d) Regulating the rate of interest on money;

(e) Concerning the settlement or administration of any estate, or the sale or mortgage of any property, of any infant, or of a person of unsound mind, or of any deceased person;

(f) The removal of the disability of infancy;

(g) Granting to any person, corporation, or association the right to have any ferry, bridge, road, or fish-trap;

(h) Exemption of property from taxation or from levy or sale;

(i) Providing for the adoption or legitimation of children;

(j) Changing the law of descent and distribution;

(k) Exempting any person from jury, road, or other civil duty (and no person shall be exempted therefrom by force of any local or private law);

(l) Laying out, opening, altering, and working roads and highways;

(m) Vacating any road or highway, town plat, street, alley, or public grounds;

(n) Selecting, drawing, summoning, or empaneling grand or petit juries;

(o) Creating, increasing, or decreasing the fees, salary, or emoluments of any public officer;

(p) Providing for the management or support of any private or common school, incorporating the same, or granting such school any privileges;

(q) Relating to stock laws, water-courses, and fences;

(r) Conferring the power to exercise the right of eminent domain, or granting to any person, corporation, or association the right to lay down railroad tracks or street-car tracks in any other manner than that prescribed by general law;

(s) Regulating the practice in courts of justice;

(t) Providing for the creation of districts for the election of justices of the peace and constables; and

(u) Granting any lands under control of the state to any person or corporation.

PROHIBITIONS

Section 91. Uniform Application of Charges and Fees

The Legislature shall not enact any law for one or more counties, not applicable to all the counties in the state, increasing the uniform charge for the registration of deeds, or regulating costs and charges and fees of officers.

Section 92. Salary of Deceased Officer

The Legislature shall not authorize payment to any person of the salary of a deceased officer beyond the date of his death.

Section 93. Retirement of Officer On Pay

The Legislature shall not retire any officer on pay, or part pay, or make any grant to such retiring officer.

Section 94. Disability On Account of Coverture Abolished

The Legislature shall never create by law any distinction between the rights of men and women to acquire, own, enjoy, and dispose of property of all kinds, or their power to contract in reference thereto. Married women are hereby fully emancipated from all disability on account of coverture. But this shall not prevent the Legislature from regulating contracts between husband and wife; nor shall the Legislature be prevented from regulating the sale of homesteads.

Section 95. Donation or Sale of State Lands; Railroad Easements

Lands belonging to, or under the control of the State, shall never be donated directly or indirectly, to private corporations or individuals, or to railroad companies. Nor shall such land be sold to corporations or associations for a less price than that for which it is subject to sale to individuals. This, however, shall not prevent the Legislature from granting a right of way, not exceeding one hundred feet in width, as a mere easement, to railroads across state land, and the Legislature shall never dispose of the land covered by said right of way so long as such easement exists.

Section 96. Extra Compensation and Unauthorized Payments Prohibited

The Legislature shall never grant extra compensation, fee, or allowance, to any public officer, agent, servant, or contractor, after service rendered or contract made, nor authorize payment, or part payment, of any claim under any contract not authorized by law; but appropriations may be made for expenditures in repelling invasion, preventing or suppressing insurrections.

Section 97. Revival of Action Barred by Limitations Prohibited

The Legislature shall have no power to revive any remedy which may have become barred by lapse of time, or by any statute of limitation of this state.

Section 98. Repealed

Section 99. Election of Officers by Legislature

The Legislature shall not elect any other than its own officers and State Librarian.

Section 100. Release of Obligation or Liability Owed to State or Political Subdivision

No obligation or liability of any person, association, or corporation held or owned by this state, or levee board, or any county, city, or town thereof, shall ever be remitted, released or postponed, or in any way diminished by the Legislature, nor shall such liability or obligation be extinguished except by payment thereof into the proper treasury; nor shall such liability or obligation be exchanged or transferred except upon payment of its face value; but this shall not be construed to prevent the Legislature from providing by general law for the compromise of doubtful claims.

Section 101. Seat of State Government

The seat of government of the state shall be at the city of Jackson, and shall not be removed or relocated without the assent of a majority of the electors of the state.

MISCELLANEOUS

Section 102. Elections for State and County Officers

All general elections for State and county officers shall commence and be holden every four years, on the first Tuesday after the first Monday in November, until altered by the law; and the electors, in all cases except in cases of treason, felony, and breach of peace, shall be privileged from arrest during their attendance at elections and in going to and returning therefrom.

Section 103. Filling Public Officer Vacancies; Compensation and Powers of Officers

In all cases, not otherwise provided for in this constitution, the Legislature may determine the mode of filling all vacancies, in all offices, and in cases of emergency provisional appointments may be made by the Governor, to continue until the vacancy is regularly filled; and the Legislature shall provide suitable compensation for all officers, and shall define their respective powers.

Section 104. Statutes of Limitation Not to Run Against State and Political Subdivisions

Statutes of limitation in civil causes shall not run against the State, or any subdivision or municipal corporation thereof.

Section 105. Repealed

Section 106. State Librarian

There shall be a State Librarian, to be chosen by the Legislature, on joint vote of the two (2) houses, to serve four (4) years, whose duties and compensation shall be prescribed by law.

Section 107. Bidding and Other Requirements for Certain Contracts

All stationery, printing, paper, and fuel, used by the Legislature, and other departments of the government, shall be furnished, and the printing and binding of the laws, journals, department reports, and other printing and binding, and the repairing and furnishing the halls and rooms used for the meeting of the Legislature and its committees, shall be performed under contract, to be given to the lowest responsible bidder, below such maximum and under such regulations as may be prescribed by law. No member of the Legislature or officer of any department shall be in any way interested in such contract, and all such contracts shall be subject to the approval of the Governor and State Treasurer.

Section 108. Termination of Duties Pertaining to Office

Whenever the Legislature shall take away the duties pertaining to any office, then the salary of the officer shall cease.

Section 109. Interest of Public Officer in Contracts

No public officer or member of the Legislature shall be interested, directly or indirectly, in any contract with the State, or any district, county, city, or town thereof, authorized by any law passed or order made by any board of which he may be or may have been a member, during the term for which he shall have been chosen, or within one year after the expiration of such term.

Section 110. Rights of Way for Private Roads

The Legislature may provide, by general law, for condemning rights of way for private roads, where necessary for ingress and egress by the party applying, on due compensation being first made to the owner of the property; but such rights of way shall not be provided for in incorporated cities and towns.

Section 111. Sale of Land by Decree or Execution

All lands comprising a single tract sold in pursuance of decree of court, or execution, shall be first offered in subdivisions not exceeding one hundred and sixty acres, or one-quarter section, and then offered as an entirety, and the price bid for the latter shall control only when it shall exceed the aggregate of the bids for the same in subdivisions as aforesaid; but the chancery court, in cases before it, may decree otherwise if deemed advisable to do so.

Section 112. Equal Taxation; Property Tax Assessments

Taxation shall be uniform and equal throughout the State. All property not exempt from ad valorem taxation shall be taxed at its assessed value. Property shall be assessed for taxes under general laws, and by uniform rules, and in proportion to its true value according to the classes defined herein. The Legislature may, by general laws, exempt particular species of property from taxation, in whole or in part. The Legislature shall provide, by general laws, the method by which the true value of taxable property shall be ascertained; provided, however, in arriving at the true value of Class I and Class II property, the appraisal shall be made according to current use, regardless of location. The Legislature may provide for a special mode of valuation and assessment for railroads, and railroad and other corporate property, or for particular species of property belonging to persons, corporations or associations not situated wholly in one (1) county. All such property shall be assessed in proportion to its value according to its class, and no county, or other taxing authority, shall be denied the right to levy county and/or special taxes upon such assessment as in other cases of property situated and assessed in the county, except that the Legislature, by general law, may deny or limit a county or other taxing authority the right to levy county and/or special taxes on nuclear-powered electrical generating plants. In addition to or in lieu of any such county and/or special taxes on nuclear-powered electrical generating plants, the Legislature, by general law enacted by a majority vote of the members of each house present and voting, may provide for a special mode of valuation, assessment and levy upon nuclear-powered electrical generating plants and provide for the distribution of the revenue derived therefrom. The Legislature may provide a special mode of assessment, fixing the taxable year, date of the tax lien, and method and date of assessing and collecting taxes on all motor vehicles. The assessed value of property shall be a percentage of its true value, which shall be known as its assessment ratio. The assessment ratio on each class of property as defined herein shall be uniform throughout the state upon the same class of property, provided that the assessment ratio of any one (1) class of property shall not be more than three (3) times the assessment ratio on any other class of property. for purposes of assessment for ad valorem taxes, taxable property shall be divided into five (5) classes and shall be assessed at a percentage of its true value as follows: Class I. Single-family, owner-occupied, residential real property, at ten percent (10%) of true value. Class II. All other real property, except for real property included in Class I or IV, at fifteen percent (15%) of true value. Class III. Personal property, except for motor vehicles and for personal property included in Class IV, at fifteen percent (15%) of true value. Class IV. Public utility property, which is property owned or used by public service corporations required by general laws to be appraised and assessed by the state or the county, excluding railroad and airline property and motor vehicles, at thirty percent (30%) of true value. Class V. Motor vehicles, at thirty percent (30%) of true value. The Legislature may, by general law, establish acreage limitations on Class I property.

Section 113. Auditor's Statement of Money Expended at Session

The auditor shall, within sixty days after the adjournment of the Legislature, prepare and publish a full statement of all money expended at such session, specifying the items and amount of each item, and to whom, and for what paid; and he shall also publish the amounts of all appropriations.

Section 114. Election Returns

Returns of all elections by the people shall be made to the Secretary of State in such manner as shall be provided by law.

Section 115. Fiscal Year; Report of Transactions; Bonded Indebtedness Limitation

The fiscal year of the State of Mississippi shall commence on the first day of July and end on the thirtieth day of June of each year; and the Auditor of Public Accounts and the Treasurer of the State shall compile, and have published, a full and complete report, showing the transactions of their respective offices on or before the thirty-first day of December of each year for the preceding fiscal year.

Neither the State nor any of its direct agencies, excluding the political subdivisions and other local districts, shall incur a bonded indebtedness in excess of one and one half (1 1/2) times the sum of all the revenue collected by it for all purposes during any one of the preceding four fiscal years, whichever year might be higher. shall compile, and have published, a full and complete report, showing the transactions of their respective offices on or before the thirty-first day of December of each year for the preceding fiscal year. Neither the State nor any of its direct agencies, excluding the political subdivisions and other local districts, shall incur a bonded indebtedness in excess of one and one half (1 1/2) times the sum of all the revenue collected by it for all purposes during any one of the preceding four fiscal years, whichever year might be higher.

ARTICLE V: EXECUTIVE

Section 116. Governor; Term of Office

The chief executive power of this State shall be vested in a Governor, who shall hold his office for four (4) years. Any person elected to the office of Governor shall be eligible to succeed himself in office. However, no person shall be elected to the office of Governor more than twice, and no person who has held the office of Governor or has acted as Governor for more than two (2) years of a term to which another person was elected shall be elected to the office of Governor more than once.

Section 117. Eligibility to Serve as Governor

The Governor shall be at least thirty years of age, and shall have been a citizen of the United States twenty years, and shall have resided in this State five years next preceding the day of his election.

Section 118. Salary of Governor

The Governor shall receive for his services such compensation as may be fixed by law, which shall neither be increased nor diminished during his term of office.

Section 119. Commander-in-Chief of Military

The Governor shall be Commander-in-Chief of the army and navy of the State, and of the militia, except when they shall be called into the service of the United States.

Section 120. Report From Officers of Executive Department

The Governor may require information in writing from the officers in the executive departments of the State on any subject relating to the duties of their respective offices.

Section 121. Convening of Legislature in Extraordinary Session

The Governor shall have power to convene the Legislature in extraordinary session whenever, in his judgment, the public interest requires it. Should the Governor deem it necessary to convene the Legislature he shall do so by public proclamation, in which he shall state the subjects and matters to be considered by the Legislature, when so convened; and the Legislature, when so convened as aforesaid, shall have no power to consider or act upon subjects or matters other than those designated in the proclamation of the Governor by which the session is called, except impeachments and examination into the accounts of state officers. The Legislature, when so convened, may also act on and consider such other matters as the Governor may in writing submit to them while in session. The Governor may convene the Legislature at the seat of government, or at a different place if that shall become dangerous from an enemy or from disease; and in case of a disagreement between the two Houses with respect to time of adjournment, adjourn them to such time as he shall think proper, not beyond the day of the next stated meeting of the Legislature.

Section 122. State of The Government; Recommending Measures

The Governor shall, from time to time, give the Legislature information of the state of the government, and recommend for consideration such measures as may be deemed necessary and expedient.

Section 124. Reprieves and Pardons

In all criminal and penal cases, excepting those of treason and impeachment, the Governor shall have power to grant reprieves and pardons, to remit fines, and in cases of forfeiture, to stay the collection until the end of the next session of the Legislature, and by and with the consent of the senate to remit forfeitures. In cases of treason he shall have power to grant reprieves, and by and with consent of the senate, but may respite the sentence until the end of the next session of the Legislature; but no pardon shall be granted before conviction; and in cases of felony, after conviction no pardon shall be granted until the applicant therefor shall have published for thirty days, in some newspaper in the county where the crime was committed, and in case there be no newspaper published in said county, then in an adjoining county, his petition for pardon, setting forth therein the reasons why such pardon should be granted.

Section 125. Suspension of Defaulting Treasurers and Tax Collectors

The Governor shall have the power, and it is hereby made his duty, to suspend alleged defaulting state and county treasurers, and defaulting tax-collectors, pending the investigation of their respective accounts, and to make temporary appointments of proper persons to fill the offices while such investigations are being made; and the Legislature shall provide for the enforcement of this provision by appropriate legislation.

Section 126. Seal of State

There shall be a seal of the state kept by the Governor, and used by him officially, and be called the great seal of the State of Mississippi.

Section 127. Commissions

All commissions shall be in the name and by the authority of the State of Mississippi, be sealed with the great seal of the state, and be signed by the Governor, and attested by the Secretary of State.

Section 128. Lieutenant Governor; Qualifications and Term

There shall be a Lieutenant Governor who shall be elected at the same time, in the same manner, and for the same term, and who shall possess the same qualifications as required of the Governor. Any person elected to the office of Lieutenant Governor shall be eligible to succeed himself in office, but no person who has been elected to the office of Lieutenant Governor for two successive terms shall be eligible to hold that office until one term has intervened.

Section 129. Lieutenant Governor as President of Senate

The Lieutenant Governor shall, by virtue of his office, be President of the Senate. In committee of the whole he may debate all questions, and where there is an equal division in the senate, or on a joint vote of both houses, he shall give the casting vote.

Section 130. Salary of Lieutenant Governor

The Lieutenant Governor shall receive for his services the same compensation as the speaker of the House of Representatives.

Section 131. Vacancy in Office of Governor

When the office of Governor shall become vacant, by death or otherwise, the Lieutenant Governor shall possess the powers and discharge the duties of the office. When the Governor shall be absent from the State, or unable, from protracted illness, to perform the duties of the office, the Lieutenant Governor shall discharge the duties of said office until the Governor be able to resume his duties; but if, from disability or otherwise, the Lieutenant Governor shall be incapable of performing said duties, or if he be absent from the State, the President of the Senate Pro Tempore shall act in his stead; but if there be no such President, or if he be disqualified by like disability, or be absent from the state, then the Speaker of the House of Representatives shall assume the office of Governor and perform the duties; and in case of the inability of the foregoing officers to discharge the duties of Governor, the Secretary of State shall convene the Senate to elect a President Pro Tempore. The officer discharging the duties of Governor shall receive as compensation while performing such duties, the compensation to which he is regularly entitled by law for service in the position to which he was elected and, in addition thereto, an amount equal to the difference between such regular compensation and the compensation of the Governor. Should a doubt arise as to whether a vacancy has occurred in the office of Governor or as to whether any one of the disabilities mentioned in this section exists or shall have ended, then the Secretary of State shall submit the question in doubt to the judges of the Supreme Court, who, or a majority of whom, shall investigate and determine the question and shall furnish to the Secretary of State an opinion, in writing, determining the question submitted to them, which opinion, when rendered as aforesaid, shall be final and conclusive.

Section 132. Contested Election for Lieutenant Governor

In case the election for Lieutenant Governor shall be contested, the contest shall be tried and determined in the same manner as a contest for the office of Governor.

Section 133. Secretary of State

There shall be a Secretary of State, who shall be elected as herein provided. He shall be at least twenty-five years of age, a citizen of the state five years next preceding the day of his election, and he shall continue in office during the term of four years, and shall be keeper of the capitol; he shall keep a correct register of all official acts and proceedings of the Governor; and shall, when required, lay the same, and all papers, minutes, and vouchers relative thereto, before the Legislature, and he shall perform such other duties as may be required of him by law. He shall receive such compensation as shall be prescribed.

Section 134. State Treasurer; Auditor of Public Accounts

A State Treasurer and an Auditor of Public Accounts shall be elected as herein provided, who shall hold their office for the term of four (4) years, and shall possess the same qualifications as required for the Secretary of State. They shall receive such compensation as may be provided by law.

Section 135. County Officers

Effective January 1, 1964, there shall be a sheriff, coroner, assessor, tax collector and surveyor for each county to be selected as elsewhere provided herein, who shall hold their office for four years and who shall be eligible to immediately succeed themselves in office, provided, however, if the offices of sheriff and tax collector are combined the holder thereof shall not be eligible to immediately succeed himself in office. The Legislature may combine any one or more of said offices in any county or counties and shall fix their compensation. The duties heretofore imposed on the county treasurer shall be discharged by some person or persons selected as required by law.

Section 136. Continuation in Office

All officers named in this article shall hold their offices during the term for which they were selected, unless removed, and until their successors shall be duly qualified to enter on the discharge of their respective duties.

Section 137. Repealed

Section 138. Selection of County Officers

The sheriff, coroner, assessor, surveyor, clerks of courts, and members of the board of supervisors of the several counties, and all other officers exercising local jurisdiction therein, shall be selected in the manner provided by law for each county.

Section 139. Removal and Appointment of County and Municipal Officers

The Legislature may empower the Governor to remove and appoint officers, in any county or counties or municipal corporations, under such regulations as may be prescribed by law.

Section 140. Election of Governor

The Governor of the state shall be chosen in the following manner: On the first Tuesday after the first Monday of November of A.D. 1895, and on the first Tuesday after the first Monday of November in every fourth year thereafter, until the day shall be changed by law, an election shall be held in the several counties and districts created for the election of members of the House of Representatives in this state, for Governor, and the person receiving in any county or such legislative district the highest number of votes cast therein, for said office, shall be holden to have received as many votes as such county or district is entitled to members in the House of Representatives, which last named votes are hereby designated "electoral votes". In all cases where a Representative is apportioned to two (2) or more counties or districts, the electoral vote based on such Representative, shall be equally divided among such counties or districts. The returns of said election shall be certified by the election commissioners, or the majority of them, of the several counties and transmitted, sealed, to the seat of government, directed to the Secretary of State, and shall be by him safely kept and delivered to the Speaker of the House of Representatives on the first day of the next ensuing session of the Legislature.
The Speaker shall, on the same day he shall have received said returns, open and publish them in the presence of the House of Representatives, and said House shall ascertain and count the vote of each county and legislative district and decide any contest that may be made concerning the same, and said

decision shall be made by a majority of the whole number of members of the House of Representatives concurring therein by a viva voce vote, which shall be recorded in its journal; provided, in case the two (2) highest candidates have an equal number of votes in any county or legislative district, the electoral vote of such county or legislative district shall be considered as equally divided between them. The person found to have received a majority of all the electoral votes, and also a majority of the popular vote, shall be declared elected.

Section 141. Choosing Governor in Absence of Electoral and Popular Vote Majorities

If no person shall receive such majorities, then the House of Representatives shall proceed to choose a governor from the two persons who shall have received the highest number of popular votes. The election shall be by viva voce vote, which shall be recorded in the journal, in such manner as to show for whom each member voted.

Section 142. Ineligibility of Legislators to Receive Certain Appointments

In case of an election of Governor or any state officer by the House of Representatives, no member of that House shall be eligible to receive any appointment from the Governor or other state officer so elected, during the term for which he shall be elected.

Section 143. Election of Other State Officers

All other state officers shall be elected at the same time, and in the same manner as provided for election of Governor.

ARTICLE VI: JUDICIARY

Section 144. Judicial Power of State

The judicial power of the State shall be vested in a Supreme Court and such other courts as are provided for in this Constitution.

Section 145. Composition of Supreme Court

The Supreme Court shall consist of three judges, any two of whom, when convened, shall form a quorum. The Legislature shall divide the state into three Supreme Court districts, and there shall be elected one judge for and from each district by the qualified electors thereof at a time and in the manner provided by law; but the removal of a judge to the state capitol during his term of office shall not render him ineligible as his own successor for the districts from which he has removed. The present incumbents shall be considered as holding their terms of office from the state at large. The adoption of this amendment shall not abridge the terms of any of the present incumbents, but they shall continue to hold their respective offices until the expiration of the terms for which they were respectively appointed.

Section 145-A. Addition of Judges to Supreme Court

The Supreme Court shall consist of six judges, that is to say, of three judges in addition to the three provided for by Section 145 of this Constitution, any four of whom when convened shall form a quorum. The additional judges herein provided for shall be selected one for and from each of the Supreme Court districts in the manner provided by Section 145 of this Constitution, or any amendments thereto. Their terms of office shall be as provided by Section 149 of this Constitution, or any amendment thereto.

Section 145-B. Further Addition of Judges to Supreme Court

The Supreme Court shall consist of nine judges, that is to say, of three judges in addition to the six provided for by Section 145-A of this Constitution, any five of whom when convened shall constitute a quorum. The additional judges herein provided for shall be selected one for and from each of the Supreme Court districts in the manner provided by Section 145-A of this Constitution or any amendment thereto. Their terms of office shall be as provided by Section 149 of this Constitution or any amendment thereto.

Section 146. Jurisdiction of Supreme Court

The Supreme Court shall have such jurisdiction as properly belongs to a court of appeals and shall exercise no jurisdiction on matters other than those specifically provided by this Constitution or by general law. The Legislature may by general law provide for the Supreme Court to have original and appellate jurisdiction as to any appeal directly from an administrative agency charged by law with the responsibility for approval or disapproval of rates sought to be charged the public by any public utility. The Supreme Court shall consider cases and proceedings for modification of public utility rates in an expeditious manner regardless of their position on the court docket.

Section 147. Reversal of Judgment for Want of Jurisdiction; Remand

No judgment or decree in any chancery or circuit court rendered in a civil cause shall be reversed or annulled on the ground of want of jurisdiction to render said judgment or decree, from any error or mistake as to whether the cause in which it was rendered was of equity or common-law jurisdiction; but if the Supreme Court shall find error in the proceedings other than as to jurisdiction, and it shall be necessary to remand the case, the

Supreme Court may remand it to that court which, in its opinion, can best determine the controversy.

Section 148. Holding of Supreme Court at Seat of Government

The Supreme Court shall be held twice in each year at the seat of government at such time as the Legislature may provide.

Section 149. Term of Office of Supreme Court Judges

The term of office of the judges of the Supreme Court shall be eight (8) years. The Legislature shall provide as near as can be conveniently done that the offices of not more than a majority of the judges of said court shall become vacant at any one time; and if necessary for the accomplishment of that purpose, it shall have power to provide that the terms of office of some of the judges first to be elected shall expire in less than eight years. The adoption of this amendment shall not abridge the terms of any of the present incumbents of the office of judge of the Supreme Court; but they shall continue to hold their respective offices until the expiration of the terms for which they were respectively appointed.

Section 149-A. Divisions of Supreme Court

The Supreme Court shall have power, under such rules and regulations as it may adopt, to sit in two divisions of three judges each, any two of whom when convened shall form a quorum; each division shall have full power to hear and adjudge all cases that may be assigned to it by the court. In event the judges composing any division shall differ as to the judgment to be rendered in any cause, or in event any judge of either division, within a time and in a manner to be fixed by the rules to be adopted by the court, shall certify that in his opinion any decision of any division of the court is in conflict with any prior decision of the court or of any division thereof, the cause shall then be considered and adjudged by the full court or a quorum thereof.

Section 150. Eligibility Requirements for Supreme Court Judges

No personal shall be eligible to the office of judge of the Supreme Court who shall not have attained the age of thirty years at the time of his appointment, and who shall not have been a practicing attorney and a citizen of the State for five years immediately preceding such appointment.

Section 151. Repealed

Section 152. Circuit and Chancery Court Districts

The Legislature shall divide the State into an appropriate number of circuit court districts and chancery court districts. The Legislature shall, by statute, establish certain criteria by which the number of judges in each district shall be determined, such criteria to be based on population, the number of cases filed and other appropriate data. Following the 1980 Federal Decennial Census and following each federal decennial census thereafter, the Legislature shall redistrict the circuit and chancery court districts. Should the Legislature fail to redistrict the circuit or chancery court districts by December 31 of the fifth year following the 1980 Federal Decennial Census or by December 31 of the fifth year following any federal decennial census thereafter, the Supreme Court shall, by order, redistrict such circuit or chancery court districts. Any order by the Supreme Court which redistricts the circuit or chancery court districts shall become effective at a date to be set therein and shall, without alteration of the composition of the districts established in such order, be enacted by the next succeeding session of the Legislature. The circuit and chancery court districts established by the Legislature prior to the approval of this amendment shall remain in force and effect until such time as they are redistricted under the provisions of this amendment.

Section 153. Election and Terms of Circuit and Chancery Court Judges

The judges of the circuit and chancery courts shall be elected by the people in a manner and at a time to be provided by the legislature and the judges shall hold their office for a term of four years.

Section 154. Qualifications for Circuit or Chancery Court Judges

No person shall be eligible to the office of judge of the circuit court or of the chancery court who shall not have been a practicing lawyer for five years and who shall not have attained the age of twenty-six years, and who shall not have been five years a citizen of this State.

Section 155. Judicial Oath of Office

The judges of the several courts of this state shall, before they proceed to execute the duties of their respective offices, take the following oath or affirmation, to-wit: "I, _____ , solemnly swear (or affirm) that I will administer justice without respect to persons, and do equal right to the poor and to the rich, and that I will faithfully and impartially discharge and perform all the duties incumbent upon me as _____ according to the best of my ability and understanding, agreeably to the Constitution of the United States and the Constitution and laws of the State of Mississippi. So help me God."

Section 156. Jurisdiction of Circuit Court

The circuit court shall have original jurisdiction in all matters civil and criminal in this state not vested by this Constitution in some other court, and such appellate jurisdiction as shall be prescribed by law.

Section 157. Exclusive Jurisdiction of Chancery Court; Transfer

All causes that may be brought in the circuit court whereof the chancery court has exclusive jurisdiction shall be transferred to the chancery court.

Section 158. Holding of Circuit Court

A circuit court shall be held in each county at least twice in each year, and the judges of said courts may interchange circuits with each other in such manner as may be provided by law.

Section 159. Jurisdiction of Chancery Court

The chancery court shall have full jurisdiction in the following matters and cases, viz.:

(a) All matters in equity;

(b) Divorce and alimony;

(c) Matters testamentary and of administration;

(d) Minor's business;

(e) Cases of idiocy, lunacy, and persons of unsound mind;

(f) All cases of which the said court had jurisdiction under the laws in force when this Constitution is put in operation.

Section 160. Additional Jurisdiction of Chancery Court

and in addition to the jurisdiction heretofore exercised by the chancery court in suits to try title and to cancel deeds and other clouds upon title to real estate, it shall have jurisdiction in such cases to decree possession, and to displace possession; to decree rents and compensation for improvements and taxes; and in all cases where said court heretofore exercised jurisdiction, auxiliary to courts of common law, it may exercise such jurisdiction to grant the relief sought, although the legal remedy may not have been exhausted or the legal title established by a suit at law.

Section 161. Concurrent Jurisdiction of Chancery and Circuit Court

and the chancery court shall have jurisdiction, concurrent with the circuit court, of suits on bonds of fiduciaries and public officers for failure to account for money or property received, or wasted or lost by neglect or failure to collect, and of suits involving inquiry into matters of mutual accounts; but if the plaintiff brings his suit in the circuit court, that court may, on application of the defendant, transfer the cause to the chancery court, if it appear that the accounts to be investigated are mutual and complicated.

Section 162. Transfer to Circuit Court

All causes that may be brought in the chancery court whereof the circuit court has exclusive jurisdiction shall be transferred to the circuit court.

Section 163. Certification of Transferred Causes

The Legislature shall provide by law for the due certification of all causes that may be transferred to or from any chancery court or circuit court, for such reformation of the pleadings therein as may be necessary, and the adjudication of the costs of such transfer.

Section 164. Holding of Chancery Court

A chancery court shall be held in each county at least twice in each year.

Section 165. Disqualification of Judges

No judge of any court shall preside on the trial of any cause, where the parties or either of them, shall be connected with him by affinity or consanguinity, or where he may be interested in the same, except by the consent of the judge and of the parties. Whenever any judge of the Supreme Court or the judge or chancellor of any district in this State shall, for any reason, be unable or disqualified to preside at any term of court, or in any case where the attorneys engaged therein shall not agree upon a member of the bar to preside in his place, the Governor may commission another, or others, of law knowledge, to preside at such term or during such disability or disqualification in the place of the judge or judges so disqualified.

Section 166. Compensation of Judges

The judges of the Supreme Court, of the circuit courts, and the chancellors shall receive for their services a compensation to be fixed by law, which shall not be increased or diminished during their continuance in office.

SECTION 167. Civil officers as conservators of peace

All civil officers shall be conservators of the peace, and shall be by law vested with ample power as such.

Section 168. Clerks of Court

The clerk of the Supreme Court shall be appointed by the Supreme Court in the manner and for a term as shall be provided by the Legislature, and the clerk of the circuit court and the clerk of the chancery court shall be selected in each county in the manner provided by law, and shall hold office for the term of four (4) years, and the Legislature shall provide by law what duties shall be performed during vacation by the clerks of the circuit and chancery courts, subject to the approval of the court.

Section 169. Style of Process

The style of all process shall be "The State of Mississippi," and all prosecutions shall be carried on in the name and by authority of the "State of Mississippi," and all indictments shall conclude "against the peace and dignity of the state."

Section 170. County Districts; Board of Supervisors

Each county shall be divided into five districts, a resident freeholder of each district shall be selected, in the manner prescribed by law, and the five so chosen shall constitute the board of supervisors of the county, a majority of whom may transact business. The board of supervisors shall have full jurisdiction over roads, ferries, and bridges, to be exercised in accordance with such regulations as the legislature may prescribe, and perform such other duties as may be required by law; provided, however, that the Legislature may have the power to designate certain highways as "state highways," and place such Commission, for construction and maintenance. The clerk of the chancery court shall be the clerk of the board of supervisors.

Section 171. Justice Court Judges; Jurisdiction

A competent number of justice court judges and constables shall be chosen in each county in the manner provided by law, but not less than two (2) such judges in any county, who shall hold their office for the term of four (4) years. Each justice court judge shall have resided two (2) years in the county next preceding his selection and shall be high school graduate or have a general equivalency diploma unless he shall have served as a justice of the peace or been elected to the office of justice of the peace prior to January 1, 1976. All persons elected to the office of justice of the peace in November, 1975, shall take office in January, 1976, as justice court judges. The maximum civil jurisdiction of the justice court shall extend to causes in which the principal amount in controversy is Five Hundred Dollars ($500.00) or such higher amount as may be prescribed by law.

The justice court shall have jurisdiction concurrent with the circuit court over all crimes whereof the punishment prescribed does not extend beyond a fine and imprisonment in the county jail; but the Legislature may confer on the justice court exclusive jurisdiction in such petty misdemeanors as the Legislature shall see proper. In all causes tried in justice court, the right of appeal shall be secured under such rules and regulations as shall be prescribed by law, and no justice court judge shall preside at the trial of any cause where he may be interested, or the parties or either of them shall be connected with him by affinity or consanguinity, except by the consent of the justice court judge and of the parties. All reference in the Mississippi Code to justice of the peace shall mean justice court judge.

Section 172. Establishment and Abolishment of Inferior Courts

The Legislature shall, from time to time, establish such other inferior courts as may be necessary, and abolish the same whenever deemed expedient. SOURCES: 1832 art IV § 24; 1869 art VI § 24. SECTION 172-A. Court order for tax levy or tax increase   prohibited. Neither the Supreme Court nor any inferior court of this State shall have the power to instruct or order the State or any political subdivision thereof, or an official of the State or a political subdivision, to levy or increase taxes.

Section 173. Attorney General

There shall be an Attorney General elected at the same time and in the same manner as the Governor is elected, whose term of office shall be four years and whose compensation shall be fixed by law. The qualifications for the Attorney General shall be the same as herein prescribed for judges of the circuit and chancery courts.

Section 174. District Attorneys

A district attorney for each circuit court district shall be selected in the manner provided by law, whose term of office shall be four years, whose duties shall be prescribed by law, and whose compensation shall be a fixed salary.

Section 175. Liability and Punishment of Public Officers

All public officers, for wilful neglect of duty or misdemeanor in office, shall be liable to presentment or indictment by a grand jury; and, upon conviction, shall be removed from office, and otherwise punished as may be prescribed by law.

Section 176. Qualifications for Member of Board of Supervisors

No person shall be a member of the board of supervisors who is not a resident freeholder in the district for which he is chosen. The value of real estate necessary to be owned to qualify persons in the several counties to be members of said board shall be fixed by law.

Section 177. Vacancy in Office of Judge or Chancellor

The governor shall have power to fill any vacancy which may happen during the recess of the senate in the office of judge or chancellor, by making a temporary appointment of an incumbent, which shall expire at the end of the next session of the senate, unless a successor shall be sooner appointed and confirmed by the senate. When a temporary appointment of a judge or chancellor has been made during the recess of the senate, the governor shall have no power to remove the person or appointee, nor power to withhold his name from the senate for their action

Section 177-A. Commission On Judicial Performance

There shall be a Commission on Judicial Performance of the State of Mississippi, to be composed of seven (7) members; three (3) of whom shall be judges of courts of record in the state which are trial courts of original jurisdiction, other than justice courts; one (1) member shall be a justice court judge; two (2) lay persons who reside in the state and who have never held judicial office or been members of the bar of Mississippi; and one (1) practicing attorney who has practiced law in the state for at least ten (10) years. All judicial members are to be appointed by the judiciary of the State of Mississippi as provided by law. Restrictions on the members of the commission may be imposed by statute. Members of the Commission on Judicial Performance not subject to impeachment shall be subject to removal from the commission by two-thirds (2/3) vote of the Supreme Court sitting en banc. On recommendation of the commission on judicial performance, the Supreme Court may remove from office, suspend, fine or publicly censure or reprimand any justice or judge of this state for:

(a) actual conviction of a felony in a court other than a court of the State of Mississippi;

(b) willful misconduct in office;

(c) willful and persistent failure to perform his duties;

(d) habitual intemperance in the use of alcohol or other drugs; or

(e) conduct prejudicial to the administration of justice which brings the judicial office into disrepute; and may retire involuntarily any justice or judge for physical or mental disability seriously interfering with the performance of his duties, which disability is or is likely to become of a permanent character. A recommendation of the Commission on Judicial Performance for the censure, removal or retirement of a justice of the Supreme

Court shall be determined by a tribunal of seven (7) judges selected by lot from a list consisting of all the circuit and chancery judges at a public drawing by the Secretary of State. The vote of the tribunal to censure, remove or retire a justice of the supreme court shall be by secret ballot and only upon twothirds (2/3) vote of the tribunal. All proceedings before the commission shall be confidential, except upon unanimous vote of the commission. After a recommendation of removal or public reprimand of any justice or judge is filed with the clerk of the Supreme Court, the charges and recommendations of the commission shall be made public. The commission may, with two-thirds (2/3) of the members concurring, recommend to the Supreme Court the temporary suspension of any justice or judge against whom formal charges are pending. All proceedings before the Supreme Court under this section and any final decisions made by the Supreme Court shall be made public as in other cases at law.

ARTICLE VII: CORPORATIONS

Section 178. Formation; Charter of Incorporation

Corporations shall be formed under general laws only. The Legislature shall have power to alter, amend or repeal any charter of incorporation now existing and revocable, and any that may hereafter be created, whenever, in its opinion, it may be for the public interest to do so. Provided, however, that no injustice shall be done to the stockholders.

Section 179. Compliance With Provisions

The Legislature shall never remit the forfeiture of the franchise of any corporation now existing, nor alter nor amend the charter thereof, nor pass any general or special law for the benefit of such corporation, except upon the condition that such corporation shall thereafter hold its charter and franchises subject to the provisions of this Constitution; and the reception by any corporation of any provision of any such laws or the taking of any benefit or advantage from the same, shall be conclusively held an agreement by such corporation to hold thereafter its charter and franchises under the provisions hereof.

Section 180. Organization

All existing charters or grants of corporate franchise under which organizations have not in good faith taken place at the adoption of this Constitution shall be subject to the provisions of this article; and all such charters under which organizations shall not take place in good faith and business be commenced within one year from the adoption of this Constitution, shall thereafter have no validity; and every charter or grant of corporate franchise hereafter made shall have no validity, unless an organization shall take place thereunder and business be commenced within two years from the date of such charter or grant.

Section 181. Taxation

The property of all private corporations for pecuniary gain shall be taxed in the same way and to the same extent as the property of individuals, but the legislature may provide for the taxation of banks and banking capital, by taxing the shares according to the value thereof (augmented by the accumulations, surplus, and unpaid dividends), exclusive of real estate, which shall be taxed as other real estate. Exemptions from taxation to which corporations are legally entitled at the adoption of this Constitution, shall remain in full force and effect for the time of such exemption as expressed in their respective charters, or by general laws, unless sooner repealed by the Legislature. and, domestic insurance companies shall not be required to pay a greater tax in the aggregate than is required to be paid by foreign insurance companies doing business in this State, except to the extent of the excess of their ad valorem tax over the privilege tax imposed upon such foreign companies; and the Legislature may impose privilege taxes on building and loan associations in lieu of all other taxes except on their real estate.

Section 182. Tax Exemptions

The power to tax corporations and their property shall never be surrendered or abridged by any contract or grant to which the State or any political subdivision thereof may be a party, except that the Legislature may grant exemption from taxation in the encouragement of manufactures and other new enterprises of public utility extending for a period of not exceeding ten (10) years on each such enterprise hereafter constructed, and may grant exemptions not exceeding ten (10) years on each addition thereto or expansion thereof, and may grant exemptions not exceeding ten (10) years on future additions to or expansions of existing manufactures and other enterprises of public utility. The time of each exemption shall commence from the date of completion of the new enterprise, and from the date of completion of each addition or expansion, for which an exemption is granted. When the Legislature grants such exemptions for a period of ten (10) years or less, it shall be done by general laws, which shall distinctly enumerate the classes of manufactures and other new enterprises of public utility, entitled to such exemptions, and shall prescribe the mode and manner in which the right to such exemptions shall be determined.

Section 183. Subscription to Capital Stock by Counties or Municipalities

No county, city, town, or other municipal corporation shall hereafter become a subscriber to the capital stock of any railroad or other corporation or association, or make appropriation, or loan its credit in aid of such corporation or association. All authority heretofore conferred for any of the purposes aforesaid by the Legislature or by the charter of any corporation, is hereby repealed. Nothing in this section contained shall affect the right of any such corporation, municipality, or county to make such subscription where the same has been authorized under laws existing at the time of the adoption of this Constitution, and by a vote of the people thereof, had prior to its adoption, and where the terms of submission and subscription have been or shall be complied with, or to prevent the issue of renewal bonds, or the use of such other means as are or may be prescribed by law for the payment or liquidation of such subscription, or of any existing indebtedness.

SECTION 184. Railroads

All railroads which carry persons or property for hire shall be public highways, and all railroad companies so engaged shall be common carriers. Any company organized for that purpose under the laws of the state shall have the right to construct and operate a railroad between any points within this state, and to connect at the state line with roads of other states. Every railroad company shall have the right with its road to intersect, connect with, or cross any other railroad; and all railroad companies shall receive and transport each other's passengers, tonnage, and cars, loaded or empty, without unnecessary delay or discrimination.

Section 185. Rolling-Stock as Personal Property Subject to Execution and Sale

The rolling-stock belonging to any railroad company or corporation in this state shall be considered personal property, and shall be liable to execution and sale as such.

Section 186. Telephone, Telegraph and Railroad Charges

The Legislature shall pass laws to prevent abuses, unjust discrimination, and extortion in all charges of express, telephone, sleeping-car, telegraph, and railroad companies, and shall enact laws for the supervision of railroads, express, telephone, telegraph, sleeping-car companies, and other common carriers in this State, by commission or otherwise, and shall provide adequate penalties, to the extent, if necessary for that purpose, of forfeiture of their franchises.

Section 187. Repealed

Section 188. Free or Discounted Tickets to Public Officers

No railroad or other transportation company shall grant free passes or tickets, or passes or tickets at a discount, to members of the Legislature, or any State, district, county, or municipal officers, except railroad commissioners. The Legislature shall enact suitable laws for the detection, prevention, and punishment of violations of this provision.

Section 189. Repealed

Section 190. Eminent Domain; Police Powers

The exercise of the right of eminent domain shall never be abridged, or so construed as to prevent the Legislature from taking the property and franchises of incorporated companies, and subjecting them to public use; and the exercise of the police powers of the State shall never be abridged, or so construed as to permit corporations to conduct their business in such manner as to infringe upon the rights of individuals or general well-being of the State.

Section 191. Protection of Corporate Employees

The Legislature shall provide for the protection of the employees of all corporations doing business in this State from interference with their social, civil, or political rights by said corporations, their agents or employees.

Section 192. Public Utilities May Be Exempted From Municipal Tax; Duration

Provision shall be made by general laws whereby cities and towns may be authorized to aid and encourage the establishment of manufactories, gasworks, waterworks, and other enterprises of public utility other than railroads, within the limits of said cities or towns, by exempting all property used for such purposes from municipal taxation for a period not longer than ten years.

Section 193. Remedy for Injury to Railroad Employee

Every employee of any railroad corporation shall have the same right and remedies for any injury suffered by him from the act or omission of said corporation or its employees, as are allowed by law to other persons not employees where the injury results from the negligence of a superior agent or officer, or of a person having the right to control or direct the services of the party injured, and also when the injury results from the negligence of a fellow-servant engaged in another department of labor from that of the party injured, or of a fellow-servant on another train of cars, or one engaged about a different piece of work. Knowledge by any employee injured, of the defective or unsafe character or condition of any machinery, ways, or appliances, shall be no defense to an action for injury caused thereby, except as to conductors or engineers in charge of dangerous or unsafe cars, or engines voluntarily operated by them. Where death ensues from any injury to employees, the legal or personal representatives of the person injured shall have the same right and remedies as are allowed by law to such representatives of other persons. Any contract or agreement, express or implied, made by any employee to waive the benefit of this section shall be null and void; and this section shall not be construed to deprive any employee of a corporation or his legal or personal representative, of any right or remedy that he now has by the law of the land. The Legislature may extend the remedies herein provided for to any other class of employees.

Section 194. Repealed

Section 195. Common Carriers Designated

Express, telegraph, telephone, and sleeping-car companies are declared common carriers in their respective lines of business, and subject to liability as such.

Section 196. Repealed

Section 197. Repealed

Section 198. Trusts, Combinations, Contracts and Agreements Inimical to Public Welfare

The Legislature shall enact laws to prevent all trusts, combinations, contracts, and agreements inimical to the public welfare.

Section 198-A. Right to Work; Labor Unions

It is hereby declared to be the public policy of Mississippi that the right of a person or persons to work shall not be denied or abridged on account of membership or nonmembership in any labor union or labor organization. Any agreement or combination between any employer and any labor union or labor organization whereby any person not a member of such union or organization shall be denied the right to work for an employer, or whereby such membership is made a condition of employment or continuation of employment by such employer, or whereby any such union or organization acquires an employment monopoly in any enterprise, is hereby declared to be an illegal combination or conspiracy and against public policy. No person shall be required by an employer to become or remain a member of any labor union or labor organization as a condition of employment or continuation of employment by such employer. No person shall be required by an employer to abstain or refrain from membership in any labor union or labor organization as a condition of employment or continuation of employment. No employer shall require any person, as a condition of employment or continuation of employment, to pay any dues, fees or other charges of any kind to any labor union or labor organization.

Any person who may be denied employment or be deprived of continuation of his employment in violation of any paragraph of this section shall be entitled to recover from such employer and from any other person, firm, corporation or association acting in concert with him by appropriate action in the courts of this state such actual damages as he may have sustained by reason of such denial or deprivation of employment. The provisions of this section shall not apply to any lawful contract in force on the effective date of this section, but they shall apply to all contracts thereafter entered into and to any renewal or extension of an existing contract thereafter occurring. The provisions of this section shall not apply to any employer or employee under the jurisdiction of the Federal Railway Labor Act.

Section 199. "Corporation" Defined

The term "corporation" used in this article shall include all associations and all joint-stock companies for pecuniary gain having privileges not possessed by individuals or partnerships.

Section 200. Enforcement of Provisions

The legislature shall enforce the provisions of this article by appropriate legislation.

ARTICLE VIII: EDUCATION

Section 201. Free Public Schools

The Legislature shall, by general law, provide for the establishment, maintenance and support of free public schools upon such conditions and limitations as the Legislature may prescribe.

Section 202. State Superintendent of Public Education

(1) Until July 1, 1984, there shall be a Superintendent of Public Education elected at the same time and in the same manner as the Governor, who shall have the qualifications required by the Secretary of State, and hold his office for four (4) years, and until his successor shall be elected and qualified, who shall have the general supervision of the common schools and and of the educational interests of the state, and who shall perform such other duties and receive compensation as shall be prescribed by law. However, an election for the Superintendent of Public Education shall not be held at the general election in 1983, and the term of the Superintendent of Public Education who was elected at the general election in 1979 shall be extended to July 1, 1984, on which date it shall expire.

(2) From and after July 1, 1984, there shall be a State Superintendent of Public Education who shall be appointed by the State Board of Education, with the advice and consent of the Senate, and serve at the board's will and pleasure. He shall possess such qualifications as may be prescribed by law. He shall be the chief administrative officer for the State Department of Education and shall administer the department in accordance with the policies established by the State Board of Education. He shall perform such other duties and receive such compensation as shall be prescribed by law.

Section 203. State Board of Education

(1) Until July 1, 1984, there shall be a Board of Education, consisting of the Secretary of State, the Attorney General and the Superintendent of Public Education, for the management and investment of the school funds according to law, and for the performance of such other duties as may be prescribed. The superintendent and one (1) other of said board shall constitute a quorum.

(2) From and after July 1, 1984, there shall be a State Board of Education which shall manage and invest school funds according to law, formulate policies according to law for implementation by the State Department of Education, and perform such other duties as prescribed by law. The board shall consist of nine (9) members of which none shall be an elected official. The Governor shall appoint one (1) member who shall be a resident of the Northern Supreme Court District and who shall serve an initial term of one (1) year, one (1) member who shall be a resident of the Central Supreme Court District and who shall serve an initial term of five (5) years, one (1) member who shall be a resident of the Southern Supreme Court District and who shall serve an initial term of nine (9) years, one (1) member who shall be employed on an active and full-time basis as a school administrator and who shall serve an initial term of three (3) years, and one (1) member who shall be employed on an active and full-time basis as a schoolteacher and who shall serve an initial term of seven (7) years. The Lieutenant Governor shall appoint two (2) members from the state at large, one (1) of whom shall serve an initial term of four (4) years and one (1) of whom shall serve an initial term of eight (8) years. The Speaker of the House of Representatives shall appoint two (2) members from the state at large, one (1) of who shall serve an initial term of two (2) years and one (1) of whom shall serve an initial term of six (6) years. The initial terms of appointees shall begin on July 1, 1984, and all subsequent appointments shall begin on the first day of July for a term of (9) years and continue until their successors are appointed and qualify. An appointment to fill a vacancy which arises for reasons other than by expiration of a term of office shall be for the unexpired term only. The Legislature shall by general law prescribe the compensation which members of the board shall be entitled to receive. All members shall be appointed with the advice and consent of the Senate and no members shall be actively engaged in the educational profession except as stated above.

Section 204. County Superintendents of Education

There shall be a superintendent of public education in each county, who shall be appointed by the board of education by and with the advice and consent of the Senate, whose term of office shall be four years, and whose qualifications, compensation, and duties, shall be prescribed by law: Provided, That the Legislature shall have power to make the office of county school superintendent of the several counties elective, or may otherwise provide for the discharge of the duties of county superintendent, or abolish said office.

Section 205. Repealed

Section 206. State Common-School Fund; Additional Tax Levy by District

There shall be a state common-school fund, to be taken from the General Fund in the State Treasury, which shall be used for the maintenance and support of the common schools. Any county or separate school district may levy an additional tax, as prescribed by general law, to maintain its schools. The state common-school fund shall be distributed among the several counties and separate school districts in proportion to the number of educable children in each, to be determined by data collected through the office of the State Superintendent of Education in the manner to be prescribed by law.

Section 206-A. Establishment of Education Improvement Trust Fund

There is hereby created and established in the State Treasury a trust fund which may be used, as hereinafter provided, for the improvement of education within the State of Mississippi. There shall be deposited in such trust fund:

(a) The state's share of all oil severance taxes and gas severance taxes derived from oil and gas resources under state-owned lands or from severed state-owned minerals;

(b) Any and all monies received by the state from the development, production and utilization of oil and gas resources under state-owned lands or from severed state-owned minerals, except for the following portions of such monies:

(i) All mineral leasing revenues specifically reserved by general law in effect at the time of the ratification of this amendment for the following purposes:

(A) management of a state leasing program;

(B) clean-up, remedial or abatement actions involving pollution as a result of oil or gas exploration or production;

(C) management or protection of state waters, land and wildlife; or

(D) acquisition of additional waters and land; and

(ii) Monies derived from sixteenth section lands and lands held in lieu thereof or from minerals severed from sixteenth section lands and lands held in lieu thereof; and

(iii) Monies derived from lands or minerals administered in trust for any state institution of higher learning or administered therefor by the head of any such institution;

(c) Any gift, donation, bequest, trust, grant, endowment or transfer of money or securities designated for said trust fund; and

(d) All such monies from any other source whatsoever as the Legislature shall, in its discretion, so appropriate or shall, by general law, so direct. The principal of the trust fund shall remain inviolate and shall be invested as provided by general law. Interest and income derived from investment of the principal of the trust fund may be appropriated by the Legislature by a majority vote of the elected membership of each house of the Legislature and expended exclusively for the education of the elementary and secondary school students and/or vocational and technical training in this state.

Section 207. Repealed

Section 208. Control of Funds by Religious Sect; Certain Appropriations Prohibited

No religious or other sect or sects shall ever control any part of the school or other educational funds of this state; nor shall any funds be appropriated toward the support of any sectarian school, or to any school that at the time of receiving such appropriation is not conducted as a free school.

Section 209. Institutions for Education of Deaf, Dumb and Blind

It shall be the duty of the Legislature to provide by law for the support of institutions for the education of the deaf, dumb, and blind.

Section 210. Sale of Public School Supplies

No public officer of this State, or any district, county, city, or town thereof, nor any teacher or trustee of any public school, shall be interested in the sale, proceeds, or profits of any books, apparatus, or furniture to be used in any public school in this state. Penalties shall be provided by law for the violation of this section.

Section 211. Sixteenth Section Lands

(1) The Legislature shall enact such laws as may be necessary to ascertain the true condition of the title to the sixteenth section lands in this State, or lands granted in lieu thereof, in the Choctaw Purchase, and shall provide that the sixteenth section lands reserved for the support of township schools, except as hereinafter provided, shall not be sold nor shall they be leased for a longer term than ten (10) years for lands situated outside municipalities and for lands situated within municipalities for a longer term than ninety-nine (99) years, for a gross sum; provided further, that existing leases of the sixteenth section lands situated in the municipalities of the State may, for a gross sum, be extended for a term of years not exceeding ninety-nine (99) years from the date of such extension, but the Legislature may provide for the lease of sixteenth section lands for a term of years not exceeding twenty-five (25) years for forest and agricultural lands and not exceeding forty (40) years for all other classifications of such lands for a ground rental, payable annually, and in the case of uncleared lands may lease them for such short terms as may be deemed proper in consideration of the improvement thereof, with right thereafter to lease for a term or to hold on payment of ground rent; provided however, that land granted in lieu of sixteenth section lands in this state and situated outside of the county holding or owning same may be sold and the proceeds from such sale may be invested in a manner to be prescribed by the Legislature; but provided further, however, that the Legislature, for industrial development thereon, may authorize the sale, in whole or in part for a gross sum or otherwise, of sixteenth section lands, or lands granted in lieu thereof situated within the county; and the Legislature shall either provide for the purchase of other lands within the county to be held for the benefit of the township schools in lieu of the lands old or shall provide for the investment of the proceeds of such sale for the benefit of the township schools, or the Legislature may provide for both purchase of other lands to be so held and investment of proceeds for the benefit of the township schools; and the Legislature, for industrial development thereon, may authorize the granting of leases on sixteenth section lands, or lands granted in lieu thereof, in whole or in part, for a gross sum or otherwise, for terms not to exceed ninety-nine (99) years, and the Legislature shall provide for the investment of the proceeds of such leases for the benefit of the township schools. The Legislature may authorize the lease sold or shall provide for the investment of the proceeds of such sale for the benefit of the township schools, or the Legislature may provide for both purchase of other lands to be so held and investment of proceeds for the benefit of the township schools; and the Legislature, for industrial development thereon, may authorize the granting of leases on sixteenth section lands, or lands granted in lieu thereof, in whole or in part, for a gross sum or otherwise, for terms not to exceed ninety-nine (99) years, and the Legislature shall provide for the investment of the proceeds of such leases for the benefit of the township schools. The Legislature may authorize the lease of not more than three (3) acres of sixteenth section lands or lands granted in lieu thereof for a term not exceeding ninety-nine (99) years for a ground rental, payable annually, to any church, having its principal place of worship situated on such lands, which has been in continuous operation at that location for not less than twenty-five (25) years at the time of the lease.

(2) Notwithstanding any limitation on the terms of leases provided in subsection (1) of this section, the Legislature may provide, by general law, for leases on liquid, solid or gaseous minerals with terms coextensive with the operations to produce such minerals.

Section 212. Interest Rate On Chickasaw School Fund and Other Educational Trust Funds

The rate of interest on the fund known as the "Chickasaw School Fund," and other trust funds for educational purposes for which the State is responsible, shall be fixed, and remain as long as said funds are held by the State, at six per centum per annum from and after the close of the fiscal year A.D. 1891; and the distribution of said interest shall be made semiannually, on the first of May and November of each year.

Section 213. Agricultural and Mechanical Colleges

The State having received and appropriated the land donated to it for the support of agricultural and mechanical colleges by the United States, and having, in furtherance of the beneficent design of Congress in granting said land, established the Agricultural and Mechanical College of Mississippi and the Alcorn Agricultural and Mechanical College, it is the duty of the State to sacredly carry out the conditions of the Act of Congress upon the subject, approved July 2, A.D. 1862, and the Legislature shall preserve intact the endowments to and support said colleges.

Section 213-A. State Institutions of Higher Learning

The State institutions of higher learning in Mississippi, to wit: University of Mississippi, Mississippi State University of Agriculture and Applied Science, Mississippi University for Women, University of Southern Mississippi, Delta State University, Alcorn State University, Jackson State University, Mississippi Valley State University, and any others which may be organized or established by the State of Mississippi, shall be under the management and control of a board of trustees to be known as the Board of Trustees of State Institutions of Higher Learning. The Governor shall appoint the members of the board with the advice and consent of the Senate. The Governor shall appoint only persons who are qualified electors residing in the district from which each is appointed, and at least twentyfive

(25) years of age, and of the highest order of intelligence, character, learning and fitness for the performance of such duties, to the end that such board shall perform its high and honorable duties to the greatest advantage of the people of the State and such educational institutions, uninfluenced by any political considerations. The board of trustees shall be composed of twelve (12) members. The members of the board of trustees as constituted on January 1, 2004, shall continue to serve until expiration of their respective terms of office. Appointments made to fill vacancies created by expiration of members' terms of office occurring after January 1, 2004, shall be as follows: The initial term of the members appointed in 2004 shall be for eleven (11) years; the initial term of the members appointed in 2008 shall be for ten (10) years; and the initial term of the members appointed in 2012 shall be for nine (9) years. After the expiration of the initial terms, all terms shall be for nine (9) years. Four (4) members of the board of trustees shall be appointed from each of the three (3) Mississippi Supreme Court districts and, as such vacancies occur, the Governor shall make appointments from the Supreme Court district having the smallest number of board members until the membership includes four (4) members from each district. In case of a vacancy on the board by death or resignation of a member, or from any cause other than the expiration of such member's term of office, the board shall elect his successor, who shall hold office until the end of the next session of the Legislature. During such term of the session of the Legislature, the Governor shall appoint the successor member of the board from the district from which his predecessor was appointed, to hold office for the balance of the unexpired term for which such original trustee was appointed, to the end that one-third (1/3) of such trustees' terms will expire each three (3) years. The Legislature shall provide by law for the appointment of a trustee for the La Bauve Fund at the University of Mississippi and for the perpetuation of such fund. Such board shall have the power and authority to elect the heads of the various institutions of higher learning, and contract with all deans, professors and other members of the teaching staff, and all administrative employees of the institutions for a term not exceeding four (4)

years; but the board may terminate any such contract at any time for malfeasance, inefficiency or contumacious conduct, but never for political reasons. Nothing herein contained shall in any way limit or take away the power the Legislature had and possessed, if any, at the time of the adoption of this amendment, to consolidate, abolish or change the status of any of the above named institutions.

Section 213-B. Repealed

ARTICLE IX: MILITIA

Section 214. Persons Subject to Military Duty

All able-bodied male citizens of the State between the ages of eighteen and forty-five years shall be liable to military duty in the militia of this State, in such manner as the Legislature may provide.

Section 215. Organization of Militia by Legislature

The Legislature shall provide for the organizing, arming, equipping, and discipline of the militia, and for paying the same when called into active service.

Section 216. Appointment and Removal of Militia Officers

All officers of militia, except non-commissioned officers, shall be appointed by the Governor, by and with the consent of the Senate, or elected, as the Legislature may determine; and no commissioned officer shall be removed from office except by the Senate on suggestion of the Governor, stating the ground on which such removal is recommended, or by the decision of a court-martial pursuant to law, or at his own request.

Section 217. Governor as Commander-in-Chief

The Governor shall be Commander-in-Chief of the militia, except when it is called into the service of the United States, and shall have power to call forth the militia to execute the laws, repel invasion and to suppress riots and insurrections.

Section 218. Major-General; Brigadier-General

The Governor shall nominate, and, by and with the consent of the Senate, commission one major-general for the State, who shall be a citizen thereof, and also one brigadier-general for each congressional district, who shall be a resident of the district for which he shall be appointed, and each district shall constitute a militia division.

Section 219. Adjutant-General

The adjutant-general, and other staff officers to the commander-in-chief, shall be appointed by the Governor, and their appointment shall expire with the Governor's term of office, and the Legislature shall provide by law a salary for the adjutant-general commensurate with the duties of said office.

Section 220. Exemption of Militia From Arrest for Certain Offenses

The militia shall be exempt from arrest during their attendance on musters, and in going to and returning from the same, except in case of treason, felony, or breach of the peace.

Section 221. Appropriations for Mississippi National Guard

The Legislature is hereby required to make an annual appropriation for the efficient support and maintenance of the Mississippi National Guard, which shall consist of not less than one hundred men for each Senator and Representative to which this state may be entitled in the Congress of the United States; but no part of such funds shall be used in the payment of said guard except when in actual service.

Section 222. Support of Mississippi National Guard by County Boards of Supervisors

The Legislature shall empower the board of supervisors of each county in the state to aid in supporting a military company or companies of the Mississippi national guard within its borders, under such regulations, limitations, and restrictions as may be prescribed by law.

ARTICLE X: THE PENITENTIARY AND PRISONS

Section 223. Repealed

Section 224. Employment of Convicts On Public Roads, Public Works or Public Levee Projects

The Legislature may authorize the employment under state supervision and the proper officers and employees of the state, of convicts on public roads or other public works, or by any levee board on any public levees, under such provisions and restrictions as it may from time to time see proper to impose; but said convicts shall not be let or hired to any contractors under said board, nor shall the working of the convicts on public roads, or public works, or by any levee board ever interfere with the preparation for or the cultivation of any crop which it may be intended shall be cultivated by the said convicts, nor interfere with the good management of the state farm, nor put the state to any expense.

Section 225. Placement of Convicts On State Farms; Prison Industries; Reformatory Schools; Good Behavior.

The Legislature may place the convicts on a state farm or farms and have them worked thereon or elsewhere. It may also provide for the creation of a nonprofit corporation for the purpose of managing and operating a state prison industries program which may make use of state prisoners in its operation. It may establish a reformatory school or schools, and provide for keeping of juvenile offenders from association with hardened criminals. It may provide for the commutation of the sentence of convicts for good behavior, and for the constant separation of the sexes, and for religious worship for the convicts.

Section 226. Hire or Lease of County Jail Inmates

Convicts sentenced to the county jail shall not be hired or leased to any person or corporation outside of the county of their conviction after the first day of January, A.D. 1893, nor for a term that shall extend beyond that date.

ARTICLE XI: LEVEES

Section 227. Maintenance of Levee System

A levee system shall be maintained in the state as provided in this article.

Section 228. Levee Districts

The division heretofore made by the Legislature of the alluvial land of the state into two levee districts — viz., the Yazoo-Mississippi Delta Levee District and the Mississippi Levee District, as shown by the laws creating the same, and the amendments thereto — is hereby recognized, and said districts shall so remain until changed by law; but the legislature may hereafter add to either of said districts any other alluvial land in the state.

Section 229. Boards of Levee Commissioners

There shall be a board of levee commissioners for the Yazoo-Mississippi delta levee district which shall consist of two members from each of the
counties of Coahoma and Tunica, and one member from each of the remaining counties, or parts of counties now or hereafter embraced within the limits of said district. and there shall also be a board of levee commissioners for the Mississippi levee district which shall consist of two members from each of the counties of Bolivar and Washington and one from each of the counties of Issaquena, Sharkey, and from that part of Humphreys county now embraced within the limits of said district. In the event of the formation of a new county, or counties out of the territory embraced in either or both of said levee districts, each new county shall each be entitled to representation and membership in the proper board or boards. and in the counties having two judicial districts and from which said counties two levee commissioners are to be elected, at least one of the commissioners shall reside in the judicial districts through which the line of levee runs.

Section 230. Commissioner Qualifications and Bond

All of said commissioners shall be qualified electors of the respective counties or parts of counties from which they may be chosen, except the one selected for the Louisville, New Orleans and Texas Railway Company; and the legislature shall provide that they shall each give bond for the faithful performance of his duties, and shall fix the penalty thereof; but the penalty of such bond in no instance shall be fixed at less than ten thousand dollars, and the sureties thereon shall be freeholders of the district.

Section 231. Election of Commissioners

The levee commissioners shall be elected by the qualified electors of the respective counties, or parts of counties, from which they may be chosen, said election to be held in the manner and at the time as may be prescribed by law. The term of office of said commissioners shall be four years.

Section 232. Duties and Powers of Commissioners

The commissioners of said levee districts shall have supervision of the erection, repair, and maintenance of the levees in their respective districts, and shall have power to cede all their rights of way and levees and the maintenance, management and control thereof to the government of the United States.

Section 233. Appropriation of Private Property

The levee boards shall have, and are hereby granted, authority and full power to appropriate private property in their respective districts for the purpose of constructing, maintaining, and repairing levees therein; and when any owner of land, or any other person interested therein, shall object to the location or building of the levee thereon, or shall claim compensation for any land that may be taken, or for any damages he may sustain in consequence thereof, the president, or other proper officer or agent of such levee board, or owner of such land, or other person interested therein, may forthwith apply for an assessment of the damages to which said person claiming the same may be entitled; whereupon the proceedings as now provided by law shall be taken, viz.: In the Mississippi levee district, in accordance with the terms and provisions of section three of an act entitled "An act to amend an act to incorporate the board of levee commissioners for Bolivar, Washington, and Issaquena counties, and for other purposes, approved November 27, A.D. 1865, and to revise acts amendatory thereof," approved March 13, A.D. 1884; and in the Yazoo-Mississippi Delta Levee District, in accordance with the terms and provisions of section three of an act entitled "An act to incorporate the board of levee commissioners for the Yazoo-Mississippi Delta, and for other purposes," approved February 28, A.D. 1884, and the amendments thereto; but the legislature shall have full power to alter and amend said several acts, and to provide different manners of procedure.

Section 234. Bills Changing District Boundaries or Taxes

No bill changing the boundaries of the district, or affecting the taxation or revenue of the Yazoo-Mississippi Delta Levee District, or the Mississippi levee district, shall be considered by the Legislature unless said bill shall have been published in some newspaper in the county in which is situated the domicile of the board of levee commissioners of the levee district to be affected thereby, for four weeks prior to the introduction thereof into the Legislature; and no such bill shall be considered for final passage by either the Senate or House of Representatives, unless the same shall have been referred to, and reported on, by an appropriate committee of each house in which the same may be pending; and no such committee shall consider or report on any such bill unless publication thereof shall have been made as aforesaid.

SECTION 235. Report by levee board

Each levee board shall make, at the end of each fiscal year, to the Governor of this state, a report showing the condition of the levees and recommending such additional legislation on the subject of the system as shall be thought necessary, and showing the receipts and expenditures of the board, so that each item, the amount and consideration therefor, shall distinctly appear, together with such other matters as it shall be thought proper to call to the attention of the Legislature.

Section 236. Levee Taxes

The Legislature shall impose for levee purposes, in addition to the levee taxes heretofore levied or authorized by law, a uniform tax of not less than two nor more than five cents an acre per annum upon every acre of land now or hereafter embraced within the limits of either or both of said levee districts. The taxes so derived shall be paid into the treasury of the levee board of the district in which the land charged with the same is situated; and the Legislature, by the act imposing said tax, shall authorize said levee boards to fix the annual rate of taxation per acre within the limits aforesaid, and thereby require said levee boards, whenever a reduction is made by them in their other taxes, to make a proportionate reduction in the acreage tax hereinbefore mentioned; but said acreage tax shall not be reduced below two cents an acre per annum; and all reductions in such taxation shall be uniform in each of said districts; but the rate of taxation need not be the same in both of them; and such specific taxes shall be assessed on the same assessment roll, and collected under the same penalties, as ad valorem taxes for levee purposes, and shall be paid at the same time with the latter. and no levee board shall ever be permitted to buy lands when sold for taxes; but the State shall have a prior lien for taxes due thereto.

The Legislature may provide for the discontinuance of the tax on cotton, but not in such manner as to affect outstanding bonds based on it, and on the discontinuance of the tax on cotton, shall impose another tax in lieu thereof; but the Legislature may repeal the acreage tax required to be levied hereby after the first day of January, A.D. 1895.

Section 237. System of Levee Taxation

The legislature shall have full power to provide such system of taxation for said levee districts as it shall, from time to time, deem wise and proper.

Section 238. Property Exempt From Levee Taxation

No property situated between the levee and the Mississippi river shall be taxed for levee purposes, nor shall damage be paid to any owner of land so situated because of its being left outside a levee.

Section 239. Publication of Itemized Account

The Legislature shall require the levee boards to publish at each of their sessions an itemized account embracing their respective receipts since the prior session, and such appropriations as have been made or ordered by them respectively, in some newspaper or newspapers of the district.

ARTICLE XII: FRANCHISE

Section 240. Elections to Be by Ballot

All elections by the people shall be by ballot.

Section 241. Qualifications for Electors

Every inhabitant of this state, except idiots and insane persons, who is a citizen of the United States of America, eighteen (18) years old and upward, who has been a resident of this state for one (1) year, and for one (1) year in the county in which he offers to vote, and for six (6) months in the election precinct or in the incorporated city or town in which he offers to vote, and who is duly registered as provided in this article, and who has never been convicted of murder, rape, bribery, theft, arson, obtaining money or goods under false pretense, perjury, forgery, embezzlement or bigamy, is declared to be a qualified elector, except that he shall be qualified to vote for President and Vice President of the United States if he meets the requirements established by Congress therefor and is otherwise a qualified elector.

Section 241-A. Repealed

Section 242. Voter Registration

The Legislature shall provide by law for the registration of all persons entitled to vote at any election and shall prescribe an oath or affirmation as to the truthfulness of the statements of every applicant concerning his or her qualifications to be registered to vote. Any wilful and corrupt false statement in said affidavit shall be perjury.

Section 243. Repealed

Section 244. Repealed

Section 244-A. Additional Qualifications for Voter Registration

The Legislature shall have the power to prescribe and enforce by appropriate legislation qualifications to be required of persons to vote and to register to vote in addition to those set forth in this Constitution.

Section 245. Elector Qualifications in Municipal Elections

Electors in municipal elections shall possess all the qualifications herein prescribed, and such additional qualifications as may be provided by law.

Section 246. Regulation of Elections

Prior to the first day of January, A.D. 1896, the elections by the people in this state shall be regulated by an ordinance of this convention.

Section 247. Securing Fairness in Party Primary Elections and Conventions

The Legislature shall enact laws to secure fairness in party primary elections, conventions, or other methods of naming party candidates.

Section 248. Remedies for Illegal or Improper Registration

Suitable remedies by appeal or otherwise shall be provided by law, to correct illegal or improper registration and to secure the elective franchise to those who may be illegally or improperly denied the same.

Section 249. Registration Required to Vote

No one shall be allowed to vote for members of the Legislature or other officers who has not been duly registered under the Constitution and laws of this State, by an officer of this State, legally authorized to register the voters thereof. and registration under the Constitution and laws of this state by the proper officers of this state is hereby declared to be an essential and necessary qualification to vote at any and all **elections.**

Section 249-A. Government Issued Photo Identification Required to Vote

(1) (a) Except as provided in subsection (2), A qualified elector who votes in a primary or general election, either in person at the polls or in person in the office of the circuit clerk, shall present a government issued photo identification before being allowed to vote.

(b) A qualified elector who does not have a government issued photo identification and who cannot afford such identification may obtain a state issued photo identification free of charge from the Mississippi Department of Public Safety. The elector must show appropriate identifying documents required by the Mississippi Department of Public Safety as provided by law.

(2) (a) An elector living and voting in a state-licensed care facility shall not be required to show a government issued photo identification before being allowed to vote.

(b) An elector who has a religious objection to being photographed will be allowed to cast an affidavit ballot, and the elector, within five days after the election, shall execute an affidavit in the appropriate circuit clerk's office affirming that the exemption applies.

(c) An elector who has a government issued photo identification, but is unable to present that identification when voting, shall file an affidavit ballot, and the elector, within five days after the election, shall present the government issued photo identification to the appropriate circuit clerk.

(3) This provision shall not be construed to require photo identification to register to vote. This provision only requires government issued photo identification for casting a ballot.

(4) The Legislature shall enact legislation to implement the provisions of this section of the constitution.

Section 250. Qualified Electors Eligible for Office

All qualified electors and no others shall be eligible to office, except as otherwise provided in this Constitution; provided, however, that as to an office where no other qualification than that of being a qualified elector is provided by this Constitution, the Legislature may, by law, fix additional qualifications for such office.

Section 251. Time of Registration

Electors shall not be registered within four months next before any election at which they may offer to vote; but appeals may be heard and determined and revision take place at any time prior to the election; and no person who, in respect to age and residence, would become entitled to vote within the said four months, shall be excluded from registration on account of his want of qualification at the time of registration.

Section 252. Terms of Office; General Election Dates

The term of office of all elective officers under this Constitution shall be four years, except as otherwise provided herein. A general election for all elective officers shall be held on the Tuesday next after the first Monday of November, A.D. 1895, and every four years thereafter; Provided, The Legislature may change the day and date of general elections to any day and date in October, November or December.

Section 253. Restoration of Right of Suffrage After Crime

The Legislature may, by a two-thirds vote of both houses, of all members elected, restore the right of suffrage to any person disqualified by reason of crime; but the reasons therefor shall be spread upon the journals, and the vote shall be by yeas and nays.

ARTICLE XIII: APPORTIONMENT

Section 254. Senatorial and Representative Districts

The Legislature shall at its regular session in the second year following the 1980 decennial census and every ten (10) years thereafter, and may, at any other time, by joint resolution, by majority vote of all members of each house, apportion the state in accordance with the Constitution of the state and of the United States into consecutively numbered Senatorial and Representative districts of contiguous territory. The Senate shall consist of not more than fifty-two (52) Senators, and the House of Representatives shall consist of not more than one hundred twenty-two (122) Representatives, the number of members of each house to be determined by the Legislature. Should the Legislature adjourn without apportioning itself as required hereby, the Governor by proclamation shall reconvene the Legislature within thirty (30) days in special apportionment session which shall not exceed thirty (30) consecutive days, during which no other business shall be transacted, and it shall be the mandatory duty of the Legislature to adopt a joint resolution of apportionment. Should a special apportionment session not adopt a joint resolution of apportionment as required hereby, a five-member commission consisting of the Chief Justice of the Supreme Court as chairman, the Attorney General, the Secretary of State, the speaker of the House of Representatives and the president pro tempore of the Senate shall immediately convene and within one hundred eighty (180) days of the adjournment of such special apportionment session apportion the Legislature, which apportionment shall be final upon filing with the office of the Secretary of State. Each apportionment shall be effective for the next regularly scheduled elections of members of the Legislature.

Section 255. Repealed

Section 256. Repealed

ARTICLE XIV: GENERAL PROVISIONS

Section 257. Commencement of Political Year

The political year of the state of Mississippi shall commence on the first Monday of January in each year.

Section 258. Credit of State

The credit of the State shall not be pledged or loaned in aid of any person, association, or corporation; and the State shall not become a stockholder in any corporation or association, nor assume, redeem, secure, or pay any indebtedness or pretended indebtedness alleged to be due by the State of Mississippi to any person, association, or corporation whatsoever, claiming the same as owners, holders, or assignees of any bond or bonds, now generally known as "Union Bank" bonds and "Planters Bank" bonds.

Section 259. Removal of County Seat

No county seat shall be removed unless such removal be authorized by two-thirds of the electors of the county voting therefor; but when the proposed removal shall be toward the center of the county, it may be made when a majority of the electors participating in the election shall vote therefor.

Section 260. Formation of New County; Changing Judicial Districts

No new county shall be formed unless a majority of the qualified electors voting in each part of the county or counties proposed to be dismembered and embraced in the new county, shall separately vote therefor; nor shall the boundary of any judicial district in a county be changed, unless, at an election held for that purpose, two-thirds of those voting assent thereto. The elections provided for in this and the section next preceding shall not be held in any county oftener than once in four years. No new county shall contain less than four hundred square miles; nor shall any existing county be reduced below that size.

Section 261. Expenses of Criminal Prosecutions; Fines, Forfeitures and Costs

The expenses of criminal prosecutions shall be borne by the county in which such prosecution shall be begun; and all fines and forfeitures shall be paid into the treasury of such county. Defendants, in cases of conviction, may be taxed with the costs.

Section 262. Asylums for The Aged or Infirm

The board of supervisors shall have power to provide homes or farms as asylums for those persons who, by reason of age, infirmity, or misfortune, may have claims upon the sympathy and aid of society; and the Legislature shall enact suitable laws to prevent abuses by those having the care of such persons.

Section 263. Repealed

263-A. Marriage Defined as Only Between A Man and A Woman

Marriage may take place and may be valid under the laws of this State only between a man and a woman. A marriage in another State or foreign jurisdiction between persons of the same gender, regardless of when the marriage took place, may not be recognized in this State and is void and unenforceable under the laws of this State.

Section 264. Qualifications of Grand and Petit Jurors

The Legislature shall, by law, provide for the qualifications of grand and petit jurors. The Legislature shall provide, by law, for procuring a list of persons so qualified, and the drawing therefrom of grand and petit jurors. After February 1, 1973, grand jurors may serve both in termtime and vacation and any circuit judge may empanel a grand jury in termtime or in vacation.

Section 265. Denial of Supreme Being Disqualification to Hold Office

No person who denies the existence of a Supreme Being shall hold any office in this State.

Section 266. Holding Office Under Federal or Foreign Government

No person holding or exercising the rights or powers of any office of honor or profit, either in his own right or as a deputy, or while otherwise acting for or in the name or by the authority of another, under any foreign government, or under the government of the United States, shall hold or exercise in any way the rights and powers of any office of honor or profit under the laws or authority of this State, except notaries, commissioners of deeds, and United States commissioners.

Section 267. Devotion of Time to Office

No person elected or appointed to any office or employment of profit under the laws of this state, or by virtue of any ordinance of any municipality of this state, shall hold such office or employment without personally devoting his time to the performance of the duties thereof.

Section 268. Oath of Office

All officers elected or appointed to any office in this State, except judges and members of the Legislature, shall, before entering upon the discharge of the duties thereof, take and subscribe the following oath: "I, _____ , do solemnly swear (or affirm) that I will faithfully support the Constitution of the United States and the Constitution of the State of Mississippi, and obey the laws thereof; that I am not disqualified from holding the office of

_____; that I will faithfully discharge the duties of the office upon which I am about to enter. So help me God."

Section 269. Repealed

Section 270. Repealed

Section 271. Consolidation of Counties

The Legislature may provide by a two-thirds (2/3) vote of the elected members of the House of Representatives and of the Senate for the consolidation of existing counties of the State, provided, however, that such counties combined must be adjoining.

Section 272. Repealed

Section 272-A. Retirement Systems

(1) All of the assets, proceeds or income of the Public Employees' Retirement System of Mississippi and the Mississippi Highway Safety Patrol Retirement System or any successor systems, and all contributions and payments made to the systems to provide for retirement and related benefits shall be held, invested as authorized by law, or disbursed as in trust for the exclusive purpose of providing for such benefits, refunds and administrative expenses under the management of the board of trustees of the systems, and shall not be encumbered for or diverted to any other purposes.

(2) Legislation shall not be enacted increasing benefits under the Public Employees' Retirement System of Mississippi and the Mississippi Highway Safety Patrol Retirement System in any manner unless funds are available therefor, or unless concurrent provisions are made for funding any such increase in accordance with a prior certification of the cost by the board of trustees of the systems based on accepted actuarial standards.

ARTICLE XV: AMENDMENTS TO THE CONSTITUTION

In General

Section 273. Amendment Process

(1) Amendments to this Constitution may be proposed by the Legislature or by initiative of the people.

Amendments

(2) Whenever two-thirds (2/3) of each house of the Legislature, which two-thirds (2/3) shall consist of not less than a majority of the members elected to each house, shall deem any change, alteration or amendment necessary to this Constitution, such proposed amendment, change or alteration shall be read and passed by two-thirds (2/3) vote of each house, as herein provided; public notice shall then be given by the Secretary of State at least thirty (30) days preceding an election, at which the qualified electors shall vote directly for or against such change, alteration or amendment, and if more than one (1) amendment shall be submitted at one (1) time, they shall be submitted in such manner and form that the people may vote for or against each amendment separately; and, notwithstanding the division of the Constitution into sections, the Legislature may provide in its resolution for one or more amendments pertaining and relating to the same subject or subject matter, and may provide for one or more amendments to an article of the Constitution pertaining and relating to the same subject or subject matter, which may be included in and voted on as one (1) amendment; and if it shall appear that a majority of the qualified electors voting directly for or against the same shall have voted for the proposed change, alteration or amendment, then it shall be inserted as a part of the Constitution by proclamation of the Secretary of State certifying that it received the majority vote required by the Constitution; and the resolution may fix the date and direct the calling of elections for the purposes hereof.

(3) The people reserve unto themselves the power to propose and enact constitutional amendments by initiative. An initiative to amend the Constitution may be proposed by a petition signed over a twelve-month period by qualified electors equal in number to at least twelve percent (12%) of the votes for all candidates for Governor in the last gubernatorial election. The signatures of the qualified electors from any congressional district shall not exceed one-fifth (1/5) of the total number of signatures required to qualify an initiative petition for placement upon the ballot. If an initiative petition contains signatures from a single congressional district which exceed one-fifth (1/5) of the total number of required signatures, the excess number of signatures from that congressional district shall not be considered by the Secretary of State in determining whether the petition qualifies for placement on the ballot.

(4) The sponsor of an initiative shall identify in the text of the initiative the amount and source of revenue required to implement the initiative. If the initiative requires a reduction in any source of government revenue, or a reallocation of funding from currently funded programs, the sponsor shall identify in the text of the initiative the program or programs whose funding must be reduced or eliminated to implement the initiative. Compliance with this requirement shall not be a violation of the subject matter requirements of this section of the Constitution.

(5) The initiative process shall not be used:

(a) for the proposal, modification or repeal of any portion of the Bill of Rights of this Constitution;

(b) to amend or repeal any law or any provision of the Constitution relating to the Mississippi Public Employees' Retirement System;

(c) to amend or repeal the constitutional guarantee that the right of any person to work shall not be denied or abridged on account of membership or nonmembership in any labor union or organization; or

(d) to modify the initiative process for proposing amendments to this Constitution.

(6) The Secretary of State shall file with the Clerk of the House and the Secretary of the Senate the complete text of the certified initiative on the first day of the regular session. A constitutional initiative may be adopted by a majority vote of each house of the Legislature. If the initiative is adopted, amended or rejected by the Legislature; or if no action is taken within four (4) months of the date that the initiative is filed with the Legislature, the Secretary of State shall place the initiative on the ballot for the next statewide general election. The chief legislative budget officer shall prepare a fiscal analysis of each initiative and each legislative alternative. A summary of each fiscal analysis shall appear on the ballot.

(7) If the Legislature amends an initiative, the amended version and the original initiative shall be submitted to the electors. An initiative or legislative alternative must receive a majority of the votes thereon and not less than forty percent (40%) of the total votes cast at the election at which the measure was submitted to be approved. If conflicting initiatives or legislative alternatives are approved at the same election, the initiative or legislative alternative receiving the highest number of affirmative votes shall prevail.

(8) If an initiative measure proposed to the Legislature has been rejected by the Legislature and an alternative measure is passed by the Legislature in lieu thereof, the ballot titles of both such measures shall be so printed on the official ballots that a voter can express separately two (2) preferences: First, by voting for the approval of either measure or against both measures, and, secondly, by voting for one measure or the other measure.

If the majority of those voting on the first issue is against both measures, then both measures fail, but in that case the votes on the second issue nevertheless shall be carefully counted and made public. If a majority voting on the first issue is for the approval of either measure, then the measure receiving a majority of the votes on the second issue and also receiving not less than forty percent (40%) of the total votes cast at the election at which the measure was submitted for approval shall be law. Any person who votes for the ratification of either measure on the first issue must vote for one (1) of the measures on the second issue in order for the ballot to be valid. Any person who votes against both measures on the first issue may vote but shall not be required to vote for any of the measures on the second issue in order for the ballot to be valid. Substantially the following form shall be a compliance with this subsection:

INITIATED BY PETITION AND ALTERNATIVE BY LEGISLATURE

Initiative Measure No. _____, entitled (here insert the ballot title of the initiative measure).

Alternative Measure No. _____ A, entitled (here insert the ballot title of the alternative measure).

VOTE FOR APPROVAL OF EITHER, OR AGAINST BOTH:

FOR APPROVAL OF EITHER Initiative No. ____
OR Alternative No. ____ A ....( )

AGAINST Both Initiative No. ____

AND Alternative No. ____ A ....( )

AND VOTE FOR ONE FOR Initiative Measure No.____
..........................( )

FOR Alternative Measure No. ____ A ....( )

(9) No more than five (5) initiative proposals shall be submitted to the voters on a single ballot, and the first five (5) initiative proposals submitted to the Secretary of State with sufficient petitions shall be the proposals which are submitted to the voters. The sufficiency of petitions shall be decided in the first instance by the Secretary of State, subject to review by the Supreme Court of the state, which shall have original and exclusive jurisdiction over all such cases.

(10) An initiative approved by the electors shall take effect thirty (30) days from the date of the official declaration of the vote by the Secretary of State, unless the measure provides otherwise.

(11) If any amendment to the Constitution proposed by initiative petition is rejected by a majority of the qualified electors voting thereon, no initiative petition proposing the same, or substantially the same, amendment shall be submitted to the electors for at least two (2) years after the date of the election on such amendment.

(12) The Legislature shall provide by law the manner in which initiative petitions shall be circulated, presented and certified. to prevent signature fraud and to maintain the integrity of the initiative process the state has a compelling interest in insuring that no person shall circulate an initiative petition or obtain signatures on an initiative petition unless the person is a resident of this state at the time of circulation. for the purposes of this subsection the term resident' means a person who is domiciled in Mississippi as evidenced by an intent to maintain a principal dwelling place in Mississippi indefinitely and to return to Mississippi if temporarily absent, coupled with an act or acts consistent with that intent. Every person who circulates an initiative petition shall print and sign his name on each page of an initiative petition, or an a separate page attached to each page, certifying that he was a resident of this state at the time of circulating the petition. The Secretary of State shall refuse to accept for filing any page of an initiative petition upon which the signatures appearing thereon were obtained by a person who was not a resident of this state at the time of circulating the petition, and an initiative measure shall not be placed on the ballot if the Secretary of State determines that without such signatures the petition clearly bears an insufficient number of signatures. The provisions of this subsection (12) shall be applicable to all initiative measures that have not been placed on the ballot at the time this proposed amendment is ratified by the electorate.

(13) The Legislature may enact laws to carry out the provisions of this section but shall in no way restrict or impair the provisions of this section or the powers herein reserved to the people.

SCHEDULE:

That no inconvenience may arise from the changes in the Constitution of this state, in order to carry the new Constitution into complete operation, it is hereby declared that:

Section 274. Laws to Remain in Force

The laws of this State now in force, not repugnant to this Constitution, shall remain in force until amended or repealed by the Legislature, or until they expire by limitation. All statute laws of this State repugnant to the provisions of this Constitution, except as provided in the next three sections, shall continue and remain in force until the first day of April, A.D. 1892, unless sooner repealed by the Legislature.

Section 275. Repeal of Laws Repugnant to Constitution

All laws of this State which are repugnant to the following portions of this Constitution shall be repealed by the adoption of this Constitution, to-wit: Laws repugnant to —

(a) All the ordinances of this convention;

(b) The provisions of Section 183, prohibiting counties, cities, and towns from voting subscriptions to railroad and other corporations or associations;

(c) The provisions of Sections 223 [Repealed] to 226, inclusive, of Article 10, prohibiting the leasing of penitentiary convicts.

Section 276. Laws Repugnant to Franchise and Election Provisions

All laws of the State which are repugnant to the provisions of Sections 240 to 253, inclusive, of Article 12, on the subject of franchise and elections, shall be and remain in force until the first day of January, A.D. 1891, and no longer.

Section 277. Laws Repugnant to Apportionment Provisions

All laws of this State which are repugnant to the provisions of Article 13, Sections 254 to 256 [Repealed], inclusive, on the subject of apportionment of Representatives and Senators in the Legislature shall be and remain in force until the first day of October, A.D. 1891, but no longer.

Section 278. Appointment of Persons to Draft Laws

The Governor shall, as soon as practicable, appoint three suitable persons, learned in the law, as commissioners, whose duty it shall be to prepare and draft such general laws as are contemplated in this Constitution, and such other laws as shall be necessary and proper to put into operation the provisions thereof and as may be appropriate to conform the general statutes of the State to the Constitution. Said commissioners shall present the same, when prepared, to the Legislature at its next regular session; and the Legislature shall provide reasonable compensation therefor.

Section 279. Continuation of Writs, Actions and Causes of Action

All writs, actions, causes of action, proceedings, prosecutions, and rights of individuals and bodies corporate, and of the state, and charters of incorporation shall continue; and all indictments which shall have been found, or which shall hereafter be found, and all prosecutions begun, or that may be begun, for any crime or offense committed before the adoption of this Constitution may be proceeded with and upon as if no change had taken place.

Section 280. Jurisdiction of Courts in Preexisting Actions

for the trial and determination of all suits, civil and criminal, begun before the adoption of this Constitution, the several courts of this state shall continue to exercise in said suits the powers and jurisdictions heretofore exercised by them; for all other matters said courts are continued as organized courts under this Constitution, with such powers and jurisdiction as is herein conferred on them respectively.

Section 281. Accrual of Fines, Penalties and Forfeitures

All fines, penalties, forfeitures, and escheats, accruing to the State of Mississippi under the Constitution and laws heretofore in force shall accrue to the use of the state of Mississippi under this Constitution, except as herein otherwise provided.

Section 282. Preexisting Bonds Remain Binding

All recognizances, bonds, obligations, and all other instruments entered into or executed before the adoption of this Constitution, to the State of Mississippi, or to any state, county, public or municipal officer or body, shall remain binding and valid, and the rights and liabilities upon the same shall be continued, and may be prosecuted as provided by law.

Section 283. Crimes and Misdemeanors

All crimes and misdemeanors and penal actions shall be tried, prosecuted, and punished as though no change had taken place, until otherwise provided by law.

Section 284. Continuation in Office

All officers — state, district, county, and municipal — now in office in this State, shall be entitled to hold the respective offices now held by them, except as otherwise herein provided, and until the expiration of the time for which they were respectively elected or appointed, and shall receive the compensation and fees now fixed by the statute laws in force when this Constitution is adopted.

Section 285. Abrogated or Repealed Laws Not Revived

The adoption of this Constitution shall not have the effect, nor shall it be construed, to revive or put in force any law heretofore abrogated or repealed.

This Constitution, adopted by the people of Mississippi in convention assembled, shall be in force and effect from and after this, the first day of November, A.D. 1890.

S. S. CALHOON, President and Delegate from Hinds County.
R. F. ABBAY, Delegate from Tunica county.
J. L. ALCORN, Delegate from Coahoma county.
R. H. ALLEN, Delegate from Tishomingo county.
D. B. ARNOLD, Delegate from Panola county.
ARTHUR ABBINGTON, Delegate from Jones county.
JNO. A. BAILEY, Delegate from Lauderdale county.
JNO. R. BAIRD, Delegate from Sunflower county.
W. L. BASSETT, Delegate from Neshoba county.
D. R. BARNETT, Delegate from Yazoo county.
T. P. BELL, Delegate from Kemper county.
J. R. BINFORD, Delegate from Montgomery county.
H. I. BIRD, Delegate from Lawrence county.
JOHN A. BLAIR, Delegate from state at large.
B. B. BOONE, Delegate from Prentiss county.
J. B. BOOTHE, Delegate from state at large.
W. A. BOYD, Delegate from Tippah county.

D. BUNCH, Delegate from Yazoo county.
R. B. CAMPBELL, Delegate from Washington county.
J. P. CARTER, Delegate from Perry county.
J. B. CHRISMAN, Delegate from Lincoln county.
C. S. COFFEY, Delegate from Jefferson county.
J. W. CUTRER, Delegate from Coahoma county.

MARYE DABNEY, Delegate from Warren county.
R. A. DEAN, Delegate from Lafayette county.
WALTER M. DENNY, Delegate from Jackson county.
GEO. G. DILLARD, Delegate from Noxubee county.
GEO. L. DONALD, Delegate from Clarke county.
G. W. DYER, Delegate from Panola county.
J. W. EDWARDS, Delegate from Oktibbeha county.
A. J. ERVIN, Delegate from Lowndes county.
W. S. ESKRIDGE, Delegate from Tallahatchie county.
W. S. FARISH, Delegate from Issaquena county.
D. S. FEARING, Delegate from Hinds county. W. S. FEATHERSTON, Delegate from Marshall county.
J. E. FERGUSON, Delegate from Newton county.
JNO. W. FEWELL, Delegate from state at large.
GEO. J. FINLEY, Delegate from Marshall county.
J. D. FONTAINE, Delegate from Pontotoc county.
T. S. FORD, Delegate from state at large.
J. Z. GEORGE, Delegate from state at large.
F. M. GLASS, Delegate from Attala county.
A. B. GUYNES, Delegate from Copiah county.
D. T. GUYTON, Delegate from Attala county.
F. M. HAMBLET, Delegate from Quitman county.
J. G. HAMILTON, Delegate from Yazoo and Holmes counties.
T. L. HANNAH, Delegate from Choctaw county.
W. P. HARRIS, Delegate from Hinds county.
T. T. HART, Delegate from Hinds county.
N. C. HATHORN, Delegate from Covington county.
JOHN HENDERSON, Delegate from Clay county.
ELLIOT HENDERSON, Delegate from Harrison county.
PATRICK HENRY, Delegate from state at large.
C. K. HOLLAND, Delegate from Calhoun county.
H. S. HOOKER, Delegate from Holmes county.
R. G. HUDSON, Delegate from state at large.
THOS. D. ISOM, Delegate from Lafayette county.
J. H. JAMISON, Delegate from Noxubee county.
D. S. JOHNSON, Delegate from Chickasaw county.
JAMES HENRY JONES, Delegate from state at large.
WALTER L. KEIRN, Delegate from Holmes county.

JAMES KENNEDY, Delegate from Clay county.
J. KITTRELL, Delegate from Greene county.
W. J. LACEY, Delegate from Chickasaw county.
ROBERT CHARLES LEE, Delegate from Madison county.
S. D. LEE, Delegate from Oktibbeha county.
T. P. LEE, Delegate from Yazoo county.
GEO. H. LESTER, Delegate from Yalobusha county.
W. F. LOVE, Delegate from Amite county.
L. W. MAGRUDER, Delegate from state at large.
E. J. MARETT, Delegate from Marshall county.
C. B. MARTIN, Delegate from Alcorn and Prentiss counties.
EDWARD MAYES, Delegate from state at large.
MONROE McCLURG, Delegate from Carroll county.
WILL T. McDONALD, Delegate from Benton county.
T. J. McDONELL, Delegate from Monroe county.
J. H. McGEHEE, Delegate from Franklin county.
G. T. McGEHEE, Delegate from Wilkinson county.
F. A. McLAIN, Delegate from Amite and Pike counties.
WM. C. McLEAN, Delegate from Grenada county.
A. G. McLAURIN, Delegate from Smith county.
A. J. McLAURIN, Delegate from Rankin county.
H. J. McLAURIN, Delegate from Sharkey county.
J. S. McNEILLY, Delegate from state at large.
GEO. P. MELCHOIR, Delegate from Bolivar county.
T. L. MENDENHALL, Delegate from Simpson county.
IRVIN MILLER, Delegate from Leake county.
ISAIAH T. MONTGOMERY, Delegate from Bolivar county.
W. H. MORGAN, Delegate from Leflore county.
J. L. MORRIS, Delegate from Wayne county.
H. L. MULDROW, Delegate from state at large.
J. R. MURFF, Delegate from Monroe county.
T. V. NOLAND, Delegate from Wilkinson county.
J. W. ODOM, Delegate from DeSoto county.
S. E. PACKWOOD, Delegate from Pike county.
J. K. P. PALMER, Delegate from Scott county.
ROBT. C. PATTY, Delegate from Noxubee county.
A. J. PAXTON, Delegate from Washington county.
C. O. POTTER, Delegate from Union county.

SAM POWELL, Delegate from DeSoto county.
J. R. PURYEAR, Delegate from Tate county.
JNO. H. REAGAN, Delegate from Leake and Newton counties.
CHAS. K. REGAN, Delegate from Claiborne county.
L. P. REYNOLDS, Delegate from Alcorn county.
L. J. RHODES, Delegate from Lee county.
W. C. RICHARDS, Delegate from Lowndes county.
S. W. ROBINSON, Delegate from Rankin county.
J. P. ROBINSON, Delegate from Union county.
J. J. ROTTENBERRY, Delegate from Yalobusha county.
J. S. SEXTON, Delegate from state at large.
JNO. M. SIMONTON, Delegate from Lee county.
H. F. SIMRALL, Delegate from Warren county.
JNO. F. SMITH, Delegate from Jasper county.
MURRAY F. SMITH, Delegate from Warren county.
W. F. SPENCE, Delegate from Hancock county.
H. M. STREET, Delegate from Lauderdale county.
T. W. SULLIVAN, Delegate from Carroll county.
E. O. SYKES, Delegate from Monroe county.
ALLEN TALBOTT, Delegate from Benton and Tippah counties.
R. H. TAYLOR, Delegate from Panola county.
R. H. THOMPSON, Delegate from Lincoln and Jefferson counties.
W. C. WILKINSON, Delegate from Copiah county.
FRANK K. WINCHESTER, Delegate from Adams county.
WM. D. WITHERSPOON, Delegate from Lauderdale, Kemper, and Clarke counties.
W. P. WYATT, Delegate from Tate county.
WM. G. YERGER, Delegate from Washington county.

Attest: R. E. Wilson, Secretary.

Delegates Who Refused to Sign the Constitution. —

Gen. William T. Martin, of Adams;
Frank Burkett, of Chickasaw; and John E. Gore, of Webster.

Delegate Absent and Not Signing. —
A. G. Webb, of Marion.

Delegate Who Died During the Convention. —
N. D. Guerry, of Lowndes.

Total, 134.